Operations of Life and Health Insurance Companies

Second Edition

Student Guide

Compiled by Nicholas L. Desoutter, FLMI, ACS, and
Jane D. Cheek, FLMI, ALHC, HIA

To accompany the textbook,
OPERATIONS OF LIFE AND HEALTH INSURANCE COMPANIES, Second Edition
by Kenneth Huggins, FLMI/M, and Robert D. Land, FLMI, ACS

LOMA®

FLMI Insurance Education Program
Life Management Institute LOMA
Atlanta, Georgia

LOMA (Life Office Management Association, Inc.) is an international association founded in 1924. LOMA's mission is to help companies in the insurance and financial services industry improve their management and operations through quality education, research, information sharing, and related products and services. Among its activities is the sponsorship of the FLMI Insurance Education Program, an educational program intended primarily for home office and branch office employees.

The FLMI Insurance Education Program consists of two levels--Level I, "Fundamentals of Life and Health Insurance," and Level II, "Functional Aspects of Life and Health Insurance." Level I is designed to help students achieve a working knowledge of the life and health insurance business. Level II is designed to further the student's career development by providing a more detailed understanding of life and health insurance and related business and management subjects. Upon the completion of Level I, the student is awarded a certificate. Upon the completion of both levels, the student is designated a Fellow of the Life Management Institute (FLMI) and is awarded a diploma.

Reprinted: July 1993

ISBN 0-939921-42-1

Printed in the United States of America

Contents

Preface

Chapter 1 Insurance Companies and Their Environment...............2

Chapter 2 Formation of Life and Health Insurance Companies.......12

Chapter 3 The Internal Organization of Insurance Companies.......24

Chapter 4 Marketing Fundamentals...............................32

Chapter 5 Agency-Building Distribution Systems..................44

Chapter 6 Additional Distribution Systems.......................60

Chapter 7 Actuarial Functions for Individual Life Insurance......70

Chapter 8 Actuarial Functions for Group and Health Insurance.....86

Chapter 9 The Underwriting Function.............................96

Chapter 10 The Customer Service Function.........................118

Chapter 11 Claim Administration..................................132

Chapter 12 The Investment Function...............................146

Chapter 13 The Accounting Function...............................158

Chapter 14 Legal Operations......................................172

Chapter 15 The Human Resources Function..........................184

Chapter 16 The Information Systems Function......................202

Chapter 17 International Operations of Life and Health Insurers..216

Chapter 18 Professionalism in the Insurance Industry.............226

Student Survey...233

Preface

Welcome to the student guide for LOMA's text, Operations of Life and Health Insurance Companies, second edition, by Kenneth Huggins and Robert D. Land. This student guide provides a comprehensive review of the topics covered in the text and is designed to help you prepare for the examination for FLMI Course 2 -- Operations of Life and Health Insurance Companies. The student guide is **not** a substitute for the text. Used properly, however, it should help you improve your performance on the examination.

Before you start working through the student guide, read the rest of this preface. It contains many practical pointers that will help you in studying FLMI educational material.

DO YOU HAVE EVERYTHING YOU NEED TO GET STARTED?

Assigned Text

Consult the current LOMA Insurance Education Catalog* to make sure you have all assigned texts. The catalog will also tell you if specific chapters are or are not assigned. If the assignment does not specify chapter numbers, then all chapters are assigned.

Study Aids

Studies indicate that students who use LOMA study aids to prepare for FLMI examinations consistently perform significantly better than students who do not use study aids. Consult the current LOMA Insurance Education Catalog for a list of other study aids for this course.

Examination Date

Check the current LOMA Insurance Education Catalog for the correct examination dates for this course. If you plan to take the examination via I*STAR, contact your educational representative. He or she can tell you what steps to follow to arrange for an I*STAR examination.

---

* The catalog is available from your LOMA Educational Representative or LOMA's Office of the Registrar.

HOW MUCH TIME DO YOU NEED TO PREPARE FOR THE EXAMINATION?

The amount of time you need to prepare for an examination depends on you -- your comfort with the material and your comfort with your own study skills. Some people spend months studying; others spend a matter of days. We can't really advise you on the length of time you need to study. However, we can offer you a few useful tips.

1. When you first begin the course, read the textbook's preface and scan through each chapter in the book. Note the learning objectives listed at the beginning of each chapter. Look at the key terms and concepts listed at the end of each chapter. These steps should help you decide how easy or difficult the material seems to you.

2. Take a calendar and figure out how many days or weeks you have until your exam. Then look at the assigned text(s) and figure out how many chapters and pages are assigned. Next, use the chart on the following page to schedule your study time. You might want to read one or two chapters a week, or you might want to read an entire book in one week. You decide. You should, however, keep these two rules of thumb in mind: (1) If you spread your study over a long period, by the time the day of the examination rolls around, you may have forgotten what you studied at the very beginning of the course. (2) If you try to compress your studies into a very short period, you may not have time to read all the material and prepare for the examination.

HOW CAN THIS GUIDE HELP YOU?

People are not born knowing how to study. Study skills are learned, and they are developed through practice and discipline. This guide is designed to help you organize your study time and master the material in the course.

Studying requires some methodical processes, but the results are worth the effort. Here's the process we recommend for each assigned chapter:

1. **Read the chapter overview printed in this study guide.** The overview will summarize the material you are about to read and put the chapter in perspective. Reading the overview will help you focus your thoughts on what you will cover in the chapter.

2. **Read the chapter objectives printed in the guide.** The objectives let you know the relative importance of the subjects covered in the chapter. Keep these objectives in mind as you read the chapter material. The test specifications that LOMA examination writers use in preparing the examinations for this course are based on the learning objectives for each chapter. If you have mastered each chapter's learning objectives you should be prepared to answer the questions on the FLMI examination.

LOMA's Stepped Schedule

for structuring your time to prepare for
the FLMI Course 2 examination
Life and Health Insurance Company Operations

Items to Study	In the boxes below, put the date on which you plan to complete each study step. Each study step includes reading the chapter overview, outline, and learning objectives, reading the chapter in the text, completing the key terms and concepts and the working outline, and answering the practice questions in the Test Preparation Guide.	In the boxes below, fill in the date you actually completed the study step.
Chapter 1 →	→	
Chapter 2 →	→	
Chapter 3 →	→	
Chapter 4 →	→	
Chapter 5 →	→	
Chapter 6 →	→	
Chapter 7 →	→	
Chapter 8 →	→	
Chapter 9 →	→	
Chapter 10 →	→	
Chapter 11 →	→	
Chapter 12 →	→	
Chapter 13 →	→	
Chapter 14 →	→	
Chapter 15 →	→	
Chapter 16 →	→	
Chapter 17 →	→	
Chapter 18 →	→	
Review Text and Student Guide →	→	
Review TPG Questions and Practice Test →		
Final Exam Date and Time →		

3. **Familiarize yourself with the chapter outline.** You know where you're headed, and you know what your objectives are. Now take a look at the framework -- the chapter outline -- the author has provided for your learning. Notice the major headings -- these are the broad subject areas covered in the chapter. Then look at the subheadings to see how the material fits together and what the important relationships within the chapter are. You may want to refer back to the outline as you read and study, and you may also use it as a review aid when you've finished the chapter.

4. **Read the chapter in the textbook at least once.** Be on the lookout for the topics, terms, and concepts that were mentioned in the introduction, objectives, and outline. Read thoughtfully and carefully, and use study techniques such as taking notes on a separate sheet, making notes in the margin of the book, and highlighting or underlining important material.

5. **Complete the "Review of Key Terms and Concepts" section in the student guide.** Terms and concepts are important building blocks within the structure of each chapter. As you master terms, your knowledge becomes more complete. Make sure you understand the meaning of each term or concept, how these terms and concepts relate to each other and to the subject of the text, and why these terms and concepts are important in the context of the subject matter being covered. If writing the definition of each term helps you learn, do that. You might also try speaking the terms and definitions into a tape player. Then you can play them back to help you learn. Or, once you are familiar with the terms, have a study partner call the terms out to you and check your understanding of them. For variety, you might also want your study partner to call out the definition for each term and ask you to identify the term. To help you locate each term in the book, we have included the page number indicating where in the text each key term or concept is first introduced and defined. Key terms are also defined in the textbook's glossary beginning on page 513.

6. **Complete the exercises in the student guide's working outline.** Each working outline consists of a series of exercises, such as fill in the blanks, matching, multiple choice, true/false, open-ended review questions, and discussion questions. Some students complete the working outline while they read each chapter as a kind of note-taking activity. Others prefer to come back to the guide and use the exercises as a self-test once they have read the chapter or a major section of the chapter. If you're not sure which works best for you, try both ways and see. Be sure to check your answers against the chapter material in the textbook.

7. **Use the Test Preparation Guide.** As noted in its Insurance Education Catalog, LOMA offers a separate publication -- a Test Preparation Guide (TPG) -- designed to enhance your test-taking

ability by providing you with practice in answering the types of questions that appear on FLMI examinations. The TPG contains a thorough introduction to test-taking, including information on how FLMI examination questions are constructed and tips for answering each type of examination question. Each TPG provides from 3 to 10 sample examination questions (and answers) for each chapter assigned so that you can test yourself after reading each chapter. Each TPG also includes a comprehensive examination similar in construction to an actual FLMI examination. This practice test gives you a chance to test yourself before taking the actual examination. (Text references and an answer key are given for the practice test.)

8. **Adapt this process to your individual needs.** You are the best judge of what will help you learn. Use the techniques that have worked for you in the past and add the study suggestions from this list that you think will help you. Ask fellow employees how they prepare for examinations.

ACKNOWLEDGMENTS

This student guide was compiled by Nicholas L. Desoutter, FLMI, ACS, and Jane D. Cheek, FLMI, ALHC, HIA. LOMA wishes to thank Robert D. Land, FLMI, ACS, for editing the manuscript and Sharon Bibee for assisting with its production.

To these individuals and to the many devoted instructors, students, and other insurance and financial services industry personnel whose constructive suggestions have been incorporated in this student guide, LOMA expresses its sincere appreciation and gratitude.

WHAT DO YOU THINK?

At the end of this student guide, you will find a survey that allows you to provide feedback directly to LOMA's Education Division staff. Your opinions, comments, and suggestions regarding the Operations of Life and Health Insurance Companies course will be vital to the development of future FLMI curriculum, textbooks, and study materials.

When you have finished your studies, please take a few moments to complete the survey. Thanks in advance for your participation.

Chapter 1

Insurance Companies and Their Environment

To help you prepare for the FLMI examination for this course, read the entire preface of this student guide. It contains many practical pointers that will help you in studying FLMI educational material. This student guide is designed to help you learn the material covered in the assigned textbook. Working the exercises in this student guide is not a substitute for reading the book. Be sure to read the assigned chapter in the book before completing the exercises in the corresponding chapter of the student guide. Consult the current LOMA Insurance Education Catalog for the correct text assignment for this course.

CHAPTER OVERVIEW

An insurance company does not exist in a vacuum. It affects and is affected by the environment in which it operates.

In Chapter 1, you read about the environment in which United States and Canadian insurance companies operate and you learned how the companies fit into this environment. You learned how insurance companies help the economy of a country and how insurance companies are affected by government regulation in the United States and Canada. Finally, you read about how the North American business environment has changed in recent years and how insurance companies have adapted to this change.

After studying this chapter, you should be able to

- Describe the role that life and health insurance companies play in a nation's economy
- Discuss the regulatory environment in which insurers operate
- Identify demographic changes and changes in economic conditions that affect the ways insurance companies operate
- Discuss how and why consumers' attitudes toward the financial services industry have changed
- Describe how insurance companies have changed their product offerings to accommodate changes in economic conditions

Outline of Major Topics Covered in this Chapter

I. The Role of Insurance Companies in an Economy
    A. General Discussion
    B. Changing Economic Conditions
        1. Inflation
        2. Policy loans, policy surrenders, and disintermediation
        3. The rising cost of health care
II. Regulation of Financial Institutions
    A. History
    B. Deregulation or Reregulation
III. Regulation of the Insurance Industry
    A. Insurance Regulation in the United States
        1. The first insurance regulation
        2. Landmark regulatory decisions
        3. State insurance departments
        4. The National Association of Insurance Commissioners (NAIC)
            a. Its purpose
            b. The zone system for company examinations
        5. The Securities and Exchange Commission (SEC)
        6. The Internal Revenue Service (IRS)
    B. Insurance Regulation in Canada
        1. History and general structure
        2. Current federal and provincial regulation
        3. The Canadian Council of Insurance Regulators
IV. Changing Populations and their Insurance Needs
    A. Maturing Population
        1. Effects of the maturing of the population
        2. Changes in the death rate
    B. The Changing Family
        1. Growing divorce rate
        2. Women and the changing family structure
    C. More Affluent and Knowledgeable Consumers
        1. General discussion
        2. Changing attitudes and consumerism
V. Technological Changes
VI. Responding to Changes and Challenges
    A. Changing Life Insurance Products
        1. Offering new products
        2. Modifying current products
        3. Enhancing in-force policies
    B. Responding to Rising Health Care Costs
    C. Reorganizing Company Operations
        1. Increased emphasis on employee authority and responsibility
        2. Subcontracting of services
        3. Changing methods of distribution

Review of Key Terms and Concepts

Define the following key terms and concepts:

level-premium whole life insurance policy (p. 5) ______________________

____

level premium (p. 5) ______________________________________

____

cash value (p. 5) ____

____

interest (p. 5) ____

____

inflation (p. 6) ____

____

disintermediation (p. 8) __________________________________

____

investment-based life insurance product (p. 16) ______________

____

mortality rate (p. 21) ____________________________________

____

universal life insurance (p. 26) ___________________________

____

health maintenance organization (HMO) (p. 28) ________________

____

preferred provider organization (PPO) (p. 28) ________________

____

WORKING OUTLINE

The Role of Insurance Companies in an Economy

1. List three roles that life and health insurers play in the economies of the United States and Canada:

   (1) ____

____

(2)____

____

(3)____

____

2. Briefly describe the services provided by deposit-type financial institutions and contractual savings institutions:

deposit-type financial institutions

____

____

contractual savings institutions______________________

____

List two other types of financial services institutions:

(1)____________________ (2)____________________

3. How do insurance companies help other businesses operate and expand?

____

____

4. As inflation rose in the 1970's, the competitiveness and profitability of level-premium whole life insurance products were challenged. Describe the effects of rising inflation on the following aspects of insurance company operations:

policy loans______________________________

____

____

policy surrenders__________________________

____

____

5. Donald Abramson surrenders his whole life insurance policy because he feels his money would be put to use better in a certain mutual fund. Mr. Abramson's action is an example of a practice which is one of the most serious problems that insurers face in times of high inflation. What is the name of this practice?

____

6. List four of the reasons that the cost of health care rose significantly between 1960 and 1990.

(1)____

____

(2)____

____

(3)____

____

(4)____

____

Regulation of Financial Institutions

7. What do we mean when we talk about "deregulation" of the financial services industry?

____

____

8. Which do you find more convincing: the arguments for or against deregulation? Why?

____

____

____

Regulation of the Insurance Industry

9. Three landmark regulatory decisions in the United States are described below. Write next to each description the name of the ruling or legislation described.

A. ______________________ This decision affirmed the role

of the individual states as the source of all insurance regulation by stating that an insurance policy was a contract of indemnity and not a transaction in commerce, and therefore not subject to federal regulation.

B. ______________________________ This decision reversed the decision described in A and stated that insurance <u>is</u> commerce and that insurance business conducted across state lines is subject to federal regulations.

C. ______________________________ This legislation declared that regulation of insurance by the individual states is in the public interest and that the U.S. Congress will leave regulation to the states as long as Congress feels that state regulation is adequate.

10. Indicate which organization is responsible for the regulatory activities listed below that affect life and health insurance companies in the United States. In the space provided, write either **"state"** for state insurance departments, **"NAIC"** for the National Association of Insurance Commissioners, **"SEC"** for the Securities and Exchange Commission, or **"IRS"** for the Internal Revenue Service.

________ Ensuring that insurance companies observe rules affecting policy reserve maintenance and investment activities

________ Reviewing the Annual Statements of insurance companies

________ Issuing certificates and licenses authorizing insurance companies to operate

________ Regulating insurance companies that market investment-based life insurance products and other nonguaranteed financial products

________ Maintaining an office for receiving and acting on consumer complaints about insurance companies

________ Assuring that insurance policy forms include the required provisions and are printed in the proper format

________ Interpreting individual and corporate tax law

________ Issuing and revoking insurance agents' licenses

________ Performing on-site examinations of insurance companies

11. Indicate whether the following statements concerning the National Association of Insurance Commissioners (NAIC) are true or false. Write **"T"** or **"F"** next to each statement.

____ The NAIC develops model bills and regulations on which states may base their insurance legislation.

____ The NAIC has the regulatory authority to require states to adopt its model bills.

____ According to the zone system for insurance company examinations developed by the NAIC, the United States is divided into four zones, and each company is examined by an examiner from the state in which its home office is located and sometimes by examiners from other states in its zone.

____ No company is ever examined by an examiner from a state which is not in the zone where the company's home office is located.

____ Each insurance company is typically examined every three to five years.

12. Indicate which organization is primarily responsible for the regulatory activities listed below that affect life and health insurance companies in Canada. In the space provided, write either **"fed"** for the federal government, **"prov"** for the provincial governments, or **"CCIR"** for the Canadian Council of Insurance Regulators.

_______ Licensing insurance companies and their agents

_______ Ensuring insurance company solvency

_______ Developing model insurance legislation

_______ Supervising the marketing of equity-based products

_______ Examining companies that are not federally registered

_______ Registering and examining federally registered companies and examining certain company financial statements

_______ Enforcing laws relating to policy contracts

Changing Populations and their Insurance Needs

13. In the following sentences, circle the word in parentheses that

correctly completes each sentence.

The average age of the populations of the United States and Canada is (higher/lower) than it was 25 years ago.

The death rate of people who are 50 to 70 years old has been steadily (increasing/decreasing).

The "traditional" family -- consisting of a husband working full-time outside the home and a wife staying home raising children and managing the household -- is becoming (more/less) common.

As a whole, the levels of education of the populations of Canada and the United States are (higher/lower) than ever before.

Technological Changes

14. Summarize some of the tasks that insurance companies are better able to accomplish because they are able to transfer information quickly and accurately.

____

____

____

____

Responding to Changes and Challenges

15. Describe some of the ways insurers have adapted their products to meet the changing demands of insurance customers.

____

____

____

____

16. List some of the steps insurers are taking to help control health care costs.

(1)____

____

(2)____

____

(3)____

____

(4)____

____

17. One way that insurance companies are responding to their changing environment is by increasing the authority and responsibility entrusted to their employees. Name three advantages to a company of such a practice:

(1)____

____

(2)____

____

(3)____

____

To assess your understanding of the material in this chapter, go to the Test Preparation Guide (TPG) for this course and work the sample questions from this chapter. The TPG will explain how to study for and take examinations and will provide you with practice in answering the types of questions that appear on FLMI examinations. Be sure to check your answers to see how well you have mastered the material covered in this chapter. If you have not mastered the material, then reread the chapter in the assigned textbook and rework the corresponding exercises in this student guide. Then return to the TPG and rework the sample questions provided.

Chapter 2

Formation of Life and Health Insurance Companies

To help you prepare for the FLMI examination for this course, read the entire preface of this student guide. It contains many practical pointers that will help you in studying FLMI educational material. This student guide is designed to help you learn the material covered in the assigned textbook. Working the exercises in this student guide is not a substitute for reading the book. Be sure to read the assigned chapter in the book before completing the exercises in the corresponding chapter of the student guide. Consult the current LOMA Insurance Education Catalog for the correct text assignment for this course.

CHAPTER OVERVIEW

There are many different forms and kinds of business, but not all of them are appropriate for selling insurance.

In Chapter 2, you learned about the different forms a business enterprise can take, and why a corporation is the only appropriate form for a life and health insurance business. You learned about the two primary types of insurance company -- stock companies and mutual companies -- and about some of the benefits and drawbacks to conducting business under each form of business. You were introduced to some of the other types of companies that sell life and health insurance. You saw how Canadian and United States insurance companies are formed. You also learned about some of the relationships that can be formed between different companies and how insurance companies can benefit from such relationships.

After studying this chapter, you should be able to

- Describe the differences between a stock insurance company and a mutual insurance company
- Explain which form of business -- a sole proprietorship, a partnership, or a corporation -- is the most appropriate for an insurer
- Compare the procedures for establishing an insurance company in the United States and Canada
- Give reasons that an insurance company would mutualize or demutualize

- Describe the differences between mergers and acquisitions
- Distinguish between a conglomerate, a spin-off, a holding company, and a subsidiary
- Define strategic alliance and give some reasons an insurer enters into one
- Identify organizations other than stock and mutual life insurance companies that can sell life insurance products

Outline of Major Topics Covered in this Chapter

I. Stocks and Mutuals
   A. Fundamental Differences
   B. Participating and Nonparticipating Policies
   C. Proportion of Stock Companies to Mutual Companies
II. The Structure of Life and Health Insurance Companies
   A. Legal Forms of Companies
   B. Incorporating in the United States
   C. Establishing Life and Health Insurance Companies in the United States
   D. Incorporating in Canada
   E. Establishing Life and Health Insurance Companies in Canada
III. Mutualization and Demutualization
   A. The Benefits of Each
   B. Difficulties of Demutualizing
IV. Mergers, Acquisitions, Holding Companies, and Strategic Alliances
   A. Mergers
      1. Definition
      2. Benefits of mergers
      3. Drawbacks to mergers
      4. The merger process
   B. Acquisitions
      1. Definitions
      2. Friendly and hostile takeovers
      3. Leveraged buyouts (LBOs)
   C. Holding Companies
      1. Definitions
      2. The trend toward holding companies
      3. Upstream and downstream holding companies
   D. Regulatory Concerns
   E. Strategic Alliances
V. Other Organizations that Market Life and Health Insurance
   A. Fraternal Benefit Societies
      1. Nature and history
      2. Characteristics of fraternal benefit society insurance
      3. Taxation of fraternal societies
   B. Banks

Review of Key Terms and Concepts

Define the following key terms and concepts:

stock insurance company (p. 32) ______

stock (p. 32) ______

stockholder (p. 32) ______

dividend (p. 32) ______

mutual insurance company (p. 32) ______

participating policy (p. 32) ______

surplus (p. 32) ______

capital (p. 32) ______

divisible surplus (p. 32) ______

policy dividend (p. 32) ______

nonparticipating policy (p. 33) ______

mutualization (p. 34) ______

sole proprietorship (p. 35)______________________________

____

creditor (p. 36)______________________________

____

partnership (p. 36)______________________________

____

corporation (p. 36)______________________________

____

charter (p. 37)______________________________

____

domestic corporation (p. 37)______________________________

____

foreign corporation (p. 37)______________________________

____

alien corporation (p. 37)______________________________

____

letters patent (p. 38)______________________________

____

memorandum of association (p. 39)______________________________

____

resident corporation (p. 39)______________________________

____

nonresident corporation (p. 39)______________________________

____

demutualization (p. 40)______________________________

____

merger (p. 45)____

____

consolidation (p. 45)____

____

economies of scale (p. 46)____

____

acquisition (p. 47)____

____

controlling interest (p. 47)____

____

friendly takeover (p. 48)____

____

hostile takeover (p. 48)____

____

tender offer (p. 48)____

____

leveraged buyout (LBO) (p. 49)____

____

subsidiary (p. 49)____

____

holding company (p. 49)____

____

conglomerate (p. 49)____

____

spin-off (p. 51)____

____

upstream holding company (p. 51)____________________________________

____

downstream holding company (p. 53)__________________________________

____

strategic alliance (p. 54)____

____

fraternal benefit society (p. 56)___________________________________

____

open contract (p. 59)____

____

closed contract (p. 59)____

____

credit life insurance (p. 60)_______________________________________

____

WORKING OUTLINE

Stocks and Mutuals

1. In the following table, put an **"X"** in the appropriate column to indicate whether the numbered description refers to stock insurance companies (stocks) or to mutual insurance companies (mutuals). Some of the descriptions may refer to both stock and mutual companies.

	Stocks	Mutuals
(1) Owned by people who purchase ownership shares in the company but who do not necessarily own policies issued by the company		
(2) Owned by the company's policyowners		
(3) The company's owners are eligible to receive a portion of the company's earnings through stock dividends		

	Stocks	Mutuals
(4) The company's owners are eligible to receive a portion of the company's earnings through policy dividends		
(5) Each of the company's owners votes for the company's directors on the basis of one vote per share of ownership		
(6) Each of the company's owners votes for the company's directors on the basis of one vote per owner		
(7) In the United States, all of these companies offer participating policies and a few can offer nonparticipating policies		
(8) In the United States, most of the policies sold by these companies are nonparticipating policies, though some of the companies offer participating policies		
(9) In Canada, these companies tend to offer both par and nonpar policies		
(10) Most newly formed life and health companies are these		
(11) In the United States, they make up 95 percent of the companies and control 55 percent of the assets		
(12) In Canada, they make up 24.5 percent of the companies and control 61 percent of the assets		

The Structure of Life and Health Insurance Companies

2. In the following table, indicate the characteristics of the three basic forms of business -- sole proprietorships, partnerships, and corporations -- by using the word in parentheses that best applies to each form of business.

	Sole Proprietorships	Partnerships	Corporations
Liability of the business's owners for the debts of the business **(limited/unlimited)**			
Continuation of the business after the death of an owner **(never/sometimes/ always)**			
Insurance companies are allowed to take this form **(yes/no)**			

* * *

The following series of questions applies to a group of investors that wishes to form a corporation in the United States.

3a. What procedure must the investors follow in order to incorporate their business in their home state of Washington?

____

3b. If their proposal is accepted by the state, what will the state do next?

____

3c. Suppose that the company also does business in Oregon. What kind of corporation is this company from the point of view of

Washington?_______________

Oregon?_______________

3d. One of the company's main rivals in Oregon is a Dutch company. What type of company is the Dutch company from the point of view of Oregon?

____

3e. If the company wants to extend its operations to Montana, what must it do?

____

3f. If the group forms a company domiciled in Washington and starts to operate in Canada, how would the corporation be referred to in Canada?

____

3g. Suppose the company is an insurance company. When the company first incorporated, it had to meet various minimum financial requirements regarding its financial surplus and the amount of premium income it had already received. What was the purpose of these requirements?

____

* * *

The following series of questions applies to a group of investors that wishes to incorporate in Canada.

3h. The group is deciding whether to do business only in Ontario or whether also to do business in Quebec and Nova Scotia. What type of documents will they have to file if they choose to incorporate

only in Ontario? ______________________________

through the federal government so they can operate in several provinces?

____

3i. If the group decides their company will operate in three provinces, how many licenses will they need to obtain

if they decide not to obtain a federal license? _______________

if they decide to obtain a federal license? __________________

* * *

Mutualization and Demutualization

4. In the following exercise, indicate in the space provided whether each advantage listed would more likely be gained by a stock company that decided to mutualize or by a mutual company that decided to demutualize. Write either **"mutualize"** or **"demutualize."**

__________ The ability to buy companies that are not in the insurance business without restricting those companies to regulations meant for insurers

__________ The ability to attract executives by offering shares in the company as compensation

_____________ The ability to avoid being taken over by other companies

_____________ The greater ability to raise capital without being limited in the ways this capital can be used

_____________ Freedom from the demands of stockholders

Mergers, Acquisitions, Holding Companies, and Strategic Alliances

5. Indicate in the space provided the type of intercompany transaction described in each scenario below. Choose from the following: a **merger (amalgamation)**, a **friendly takeover**, a **hostile takeover**, a **leveraged buy-out (LBO)**, a **spin-off**, an **upstream holding company** arrangement, a **downstream holding company** arrangement, and a **strategic alliance**.

_____________ The Shag Company creates another company, the Pile Company, which owns Shag and also purchases other companies.

_____________ The Coastal Financial Services Company makes a tender offer in order to try to gain a controlling interest in the Inland Life Insurance Company. The management of Inland discourages the company's stockholders from accepting the offer but Coastal gains control of enough stock to control Inland. The purchase of the stock is made primarily with Coastal's own assets.

_____________ The Loire Life Insurance Company, a European company, and the Amiable Life Insurance Company, a North American company, have an agreement whereby the two cooperate in order that each may learn about business in the other's primary market. The arrangement does not decrease either company's independence.

_____________ The Cactus Life Insurance Company, which is struggling financially, agrees to be absorbed by the financially healthy Desert Sand Life Insurance company.

_____________ The Round Company acquires the Square Company by borrowing 90 percent of the purchase price.

_____________ The group insurance division of Border Life becomes a separate company.

_____________ The Brick Company creates the Mortar Company. Brick owns Mortar and Mortar acquires other companies.

____________ The Red Company purchases a controlling interest in the Blue Company. The Blue Company agrees to the purchase, and the purchase is made primarily with the Red Company's own assets.

6. What are economies of scale and how do they benefit companies that merge?

____

____

Other Organizations that Market Life and Health Insurance

7. Indicate whether the following statements about noninsurance companies that market life and health insurance are true or false. Write **"T"** or **"F"** next to each statement.

____ The charter, constitution, and bylaws of a fraternal benefit society are part of any insurance contract issued by the society and any amendments to them automatically become amendments to the contract, unless any such amendment would reduce the benefits payable under the contract.

____ Fraternal benefit societies are taxed more heavily than stock and mutual insurers in both Canada and the United States.

____ In the state of Delaware, there is an organization owned by savings banks that is authorized to sell life insurance.

____ The amount of savings bank life insurance (SBLI) that a person can buy in the states of Connecticut, Massachusetts, and New York is limited in each state to a certain maximum.

To assess your understanding of the material in this chapter, go to the Test Preparation Guide (TPG) for this course and work the sample questions from this chapter. The TPG will explain how to study for and take examinations and will provide you with practice in answering the types of questions that appear on FLMI examinations. Be sure to check your answers to see how well you have mastered the material covered in this chapter. If you have not mastered the material, then reread the chapter in the assigned textbook and rework the corresponding exercises in this student guide. Then return to the TPG and rework the sample questions provided.

Chapter 3

The Internal Organization of Insurance Companies

To help you prepare for the FLMI examination for this course, read the entire preface of this student guide. It contains many practical pointers that will help you in studying FLMI educational material. This student guide is designed to help you learn the material covered in the assigned textbook. Working the exercises in this student guide is not a substitute for reading the book. Be sure to read the assigned chapter in the book before completing the exercises in the corresponding chapter of the student guide. Consult the current LOMA Insurance Education Catalog for the correct text assignment for this course.

CHAPTER OVERVIEW

To a great extent, the way that a company is organized dictates the way that it functions. In this chapter, you learned about various ways that insurance companies are organized.

You first learned about some of the principles that are essential to understanding an organization. You were introduced to the general pyramidal structure that is found in many corporations, including insurance companies. You read about several aspects of the pyramidal structure that vary from company to company, such as span of control, the extent of line and staff authority, and the amount of centralization or decentralization. You read about some of the common characteristics upon which an organization's structure can be based; for example, you encountered organization by function, product, and territory, and organization into profit centers. You learned about committees of the Board of Directors and interdepartmental committees. And, finally, you were introduced to the functional areas that are generally found in life and health insurance companies and to the responsibilities these functional areas fulfill.

After studying this chapter, you should be able to

- Describe five factors that are essential in order for a company to operate effectively
- Explain how organization charts can differ among companies and what a company's organization chart can tell you about the management style
- Describe the kind of authority that exists at each level of an organizational pyramid

- Compare and contrast the duties of a company's board of directors, officers, managers, and supervisors

- Distinguish between line and staff units

- Describe the differences among companies organized by function, product, territory, and profit center

- Explain why committees are important to a company's operations

- Describe the functions performed by the typical departments of a life and health insurance company

Outline of Major Topics Covered in this Chapter

I. Essential Organizational Factors
II. Components of the Organization and Organizational Structure
    A. Organization Charts
    B. Pyramidal Structure and Levels of Authority
        1. Policyowners or stockholders
        2. Board of directors
        3. Company management
        4. Variations among companies
    C. Span of Control
        1. Definition of span of control, factors affecting span of control, and unity of command
        2. Tall pyramids and flat pyramids
            a. Benefits and drawbacks of tall and flat pyramids
            b. Diamond-shaped organizational structures
    D. Line and Staff Units
        1. Definitions of line units and staff units
        2. Line authority and staff authority
    E. Centralized and Decentralized Organizations
III. Typical Organizational Structures
    A. Organization by Function
    B. Organization by Product
    C. Organization by Territory
    D. Organization into Profit Centers
IV. Committees
    A. Types and uses of committees
    B. Committees of the Board of Directors
        1. Executive committee
        2. Investment committee
        3. Audit committee
        4. Tax committee
    C. Interdepartmental Committees
        1. Marketing committee
        2. Budget committee
        3. Corporate communications committee
        4. Research committee
        5. Human resources committees

V. Functional Areas in a Life and Health Insurance Company
   A. Marketing
   B. Actuarial
   C. Underwriting
   D. Customer Service
   E. Claim Administration
   F. Investments
   G. Accounting
   H. Legal
   I. Human Resources
   J. Information Systems

VI. Relationships Among Company Departments

Review of Key Terms and Concepts

Define the following key terms and concepts:

responsibility (p. 64) ____________________

____

authority (p. 64) ____________________

____

accountability (p. 64) ____________________

____

delegation (p. 64) ____________________

____

coordination (p. 64) ____________________

____

organization chart (p. 65) ____________________

____

board of directors (p. 67) ____________________

____

inside director (p. 68) ____________________

____

outside director (p. 68) ____________________

____

span of control (p. 71)____________________

unity of command (p. 72)____________________

line unit (p. 76)____________________

staff unit (p. 76)____________________

line authority (p. 76)____________________

staff authority (p. 77)____________________

subsidiary (p. 82)____________________

profit center (p. 82)____________________

service center (p. 82)____________________

strategic business unit (SBU) (p. 82)____________________

matrix structure (p. 85)____________________

strategic planning (p. 86)____________________

external audit (p. 86)____________________

internal audit (p. 86)____

____

WORKING OUTLINE

Essential Organizational Factors

1. Indicate in the space provided which of the five essential organizational factors -- **responsibility, authority, accountability, delegation**, and **coordination** -- is described in each of the following scenarios. The scenarios concern the underwriting department of an insurance company and Mr. Jackson, the manager of the department.

   ________________ The department is properly organized to allow the tasks performed by the department to follow smoothly one after the other so that the department's primary goal -- prompt and accurate processing of all applications -- can be met.

   ________________ The members of the department understand clearly the goals for which they are answerable to Mr. Jackson, and Mr. Jackson understands clearly the goals for which he is answerable to his superiors.

   ________________ The members of the department have a good understanding of what tasks they are expected to carry out.

   ________________ Mr. Jackson is allowed by the company to hire the number of underwriters and other employees necessary to meet the department's goals.

   ________________ Mr. Jackson is very good at assigning responsibility for making certain decisions to certain of his subordinates, even if he is ultimately answerable for the decisions. For example, his employees only need bring the most difficult underwriting decisions to his attention.

Components of the Organization and Organizational Structure

2. Indicate what level of authority in an insurance company's organization chart is described in each of the following descriptions. Choose from the following: **stockholders** or **policyowners,** the **board of directors,** the **president, vice presidents**, and **managers.**

_______________ Generally in charge of a division of the company

_______________ Responsibilities include: setting the company's major policies; authorizing major transactions, such as mergers and acquisitions; declaring dividends; appointing the company's officers and determining their compensation

_______________ Generally in charge of a department within a division

_______________ Theoretically at the top of the organization chart but not shown on most organization charts

_______________ Directly below the top level of the organization chart

3. In the exercise below, indicate whether each manager described should have a relatively **broad** or a relatively **narrow** span of control.

_______________ Manager A's subordinates are highly skilled and competent

_______________ Manager B has not been a manager for long and has not had much time to develop management skills

_______________ Each project Manager C's subordinates work on is unique, and each is frequently very complex

_______________ Manager D's department consistently experiences a high rate of employee turnover and employees are frequently new and inexperienced

4. Determine whether the following statements are true or false. Write **"T"** or **"F"** next to each statement.

____ An organization that wanted to hold down the total amount spent on supervisory salaries could do so by having a tall organizational structure.

____ An organization that wanted to allow its managers to have closer control over the work of direct subordinates would most likely do so by choosing a tall organizational structure.

____ Common staff units of an insurance company include the marketing, actuarial, and underwriting departments.

____ Managers of staff units exercise both line and staff authority.

____ In a centralized organization, authority for many types of decisions is delegated by upper-level management to lower-level employees.

____ An organization which is strongly concerned that its policies and actions be consistent would most likely choose to centralize, but one that wants its managers to be able to respond to situations quickly would most likely choose to decentralize.

Typical Organizational Structures

5. Indicate the type of insurance company organizational structure that would be most likely to have an employee with each of the titles listed below. Choose from the following: a company **organized by function**, one **organized by product**, and one **organized by territory**.

   (1) Vice President for the Western Provinces -- ____________________

   (2) Vice President in charge of Customer Service -- ________________

   (3) Vice President in charge of Group Insurance -- _________________

6. List two potential benefits and one potential drawback of organization into profit centers.

   Benefit ____

   ____

   Benefit ____

   ____

   Drawback ____

   ____

7. Describe the purpose of a matrix structure and indicate the effect of this type of structure on the unity-of-command principle.

   ____

   ____

   ____

8. Give the names of the committees of the Board of Directors that would most likely fulfill the functions listed below.

   ________________ Dealing with the company's overall policies and with strategic planning

________________ Determining the company's broad investment policy

________________ Supervising the company's accounting and auditing activities

________________ Analyzing tax legislation and the tax implications of company activities

9. Give the names of the interdepartmental committees that would most likely fulfill the functions listed below.

________________ Using marketing information to make decisions about the design, creation, and use of products

________________ Preparing the company's annual operating budget

________________ Reviewing the company's policies on advertising and publicity

________________ Analyzing the company's own products and practices and comparing them to those of other companies

________________ Developing policies concerning the handling and compensation of employees and administering retirement plans

To assess your understanding of the material in this chapter, go to the Test Preparation Guide (TPG) for this course and work the sample questions from this chapter. The TPG will explain how to study for and take examinations and will provide you with practice in answering the types of questions that appear on FLMI examinations. Be sure to check your answers to see how well you have mastered the material covered in this chapter. If you have not mastered the material, then reread the chapter in the assigned textbook and rework the corresponding exercises in this student guide. Then return to the TPG and rework the sample questions provided.

Chapter 4

Marketing Fundamentals

To help you prepare for the FLMI examination for this course, read the entire preface of this student guide. It contains many practical pointers that will help you in studying FLMI educational material. This student guide is designed to help you learn the material covered in the assigned textbook. Working the exercises in this student guide is not a substitute for reading the book. Be sure to read the assigned chapter in the book before completing the exercises in the corresponding chapter of the student guide. Consult the current LOMA Insurance Education Catalog for the correct text assignment for this course.

CHAPTER OVERVIEW

In today's competitive environment, the success of an insurance company's marketing efforts is essential to the overall success of the company. In this chapter, we introduced you to some marketing activities that must be carried out so that an insurance company can successfully deliver products that meet its customers' needs.

You learned about the importance of a marketing plan and about the factors that determine the nature of a company's marketing plan. You also learned about how companies identify markets for their products. You read about the process that a company and its employees go through when they develop a new product. And you saw how insurance agents can make sure that customers get what they need, by helping them buy appropriate products and by providing effective customer service.

After studying this chapter, you should be able to

- Describe the purpose of the marketing function in a life and health insurance company
- Contrast market-driven and product-driven organizations
- Explain the importance of a marketing plan and identify the internal and external factors that affect it
- Name three different sources of marketing intelligence
- Compare and contrast market segmentation and target marketing
- Describe the product development process

- Describe the role of the agent in marketing insurance products
- Identify selling practices in which agents may not engage
- Explain the importance of the conservation of business and describe agents' efforts to conserve business

Outline of Major Topics Covered in this Chapter

I. Definition of Marketing
II. Market-Driven Versus Product-Driven Organizations
III. Marketing Functions
IV. Planning and Controlling
    A. Definition of Marketing Plan and Marketing Mix
    B. Developing the Marketing Plan
    C. Factors Affecting the Marketing Plan
        1. Internal factors
            a. Products
            b. Markets
            c. Current distribution systems
            d. Corporate culture
            e. Company finances
            f. Technological resources
        2. External factors
            a. Economic environment
            b. Competition
            c. Regulatory environment
            d. Societal environment
    D. Allocation of Marketing Resources
V. Marketing Intelligence
    A. Sources of Information
    B. Applications of Marketing Intelligence
VI. Market Identification
    A. Market Segmentation
    B. Target Marketing
VII. Product Development
    A. Idea Development and Product Proposals
    B. Technical Design
    C. Implementation
    D. Test Marketing and Sales Monitoring
VIII. The Role of the Agent
    A. Agent's Offices
    B. Producing New Business
        1. Prospecting and beginning the sales process
        2. Insurance for personal needs
            a. Single-need selling
            b. Total-needs programming
            c. Estate planning
        3. Prohibited practices

C. Conservation of Business
   1. Definitions of conservation and persistency
   2. Conservation at the time of sale
   3. Conservation in anticipation of lapse
D. Service to Policyowners

Review of Key Terms and Concepts

Define the following key terms and concepts:

marketing (p. 95)________________________________

____

market (p. 97)________________________________

____

marketing plan (p. 98)____________________________

____

marketing mix (p. 98)____________________________

____

corporate culture (p. 103)________________________

____

demographics (p. 105)____________________________

____

market segmentation (p. 109)______________________

____

market segment (p. 109)__________________________

____

target marketing (p. 110)_________________________

____

target market (p. 110)___________________________

____

test marketing (p. 114)____

field force (p. 115)____

detached agent (p. 115)____

prospect (p. 116)____

prospecting (p. 116)____

single-need selling (p. 117)____

total-needs programming (p. 118)____

estate planning (p. 119)____

misrepresentation (p. 120)____

twisting (p. 122)____

guaranteeing policy dividends (p. 122)____

rebating (p. 122)____

conservation (p. 122)____ persistency (p. 122)______________________________________

____

orphan (p. 125)____

____

WORKING OUTLINE

Market-Driven Versus Product-Driven Organizations

1. Summarize the characteristics of product-driven and market-driven organizations, paying particular attention to the role of the marketing department in each.

   product-driven______________________________________

   ____

   ____

   market-driven_______________________________________

   ____

   ____

Planning and Controlling

2. A company's marketing plan outlines goals for each of the company's products and the strategies it intends to follow in order to accomplish those goals. Describe, in your own words, how each of the following internal or external factors might affect the final form of a company's marketing plan. It may help you to think how these factors affect your own company.

   Internal factors

   Existing products_______________________________________

   ____

   ____

   ____

   Existing markets____

   ____

Current distribution systems

Corporate culture

Company finances

Technological resources

External factors

Economic environment

Competition

Regulatory environment______________________________

____

____

____

Societal environment______________________________

____

____

____

Marketing Intelligence

3. Describe the type of intelligence or information that insurance companies can obtain from the following sources:

their own internal reports______________________________

____

____

their agents______________________________

____

____

consumers______________________________

____

____

LIMRA______________________________

____

____

LOMA______________________________

____

____

ACLI ____

____

____

CLHIA ____

____

____

governmental authorities ______________________________

____

____

Market Identification

4. Several insurance market segments are described below. Identification of each market segment is derived by a combination of two market segmentation methods. Name the two market segmentation methods used in each case. A segmentation method may be used more than once.

Market: People in the province of British Columbia who have previously purchased life insurance through the mail.

A) ______________ segmentation and ______________ segmentation

Market: People between the ages of 25 and 40 who are strongly concerned about preservation of the environment.

B) ______________ segmentation and ______________ segmentation

Market: Affluent, middle-aged, married people who have at least two children and who are customers of investment institutions.

C) ______________ segmentation and ______________ segmentation

5. Assume that three different insurance companies are marketing new products. Identify, from the descriptions below, the type of target marketing strategy employed by each. Each is using either **undifferentiated (mass) marketing, concentrated marketing,** or **differentiated marketing.** The descriptions may refer to question 4 above.

________________ The first company has one new product and considers the product's market to be the entire population of North America.

______________ The second company is offering three new products, each designed to satisfy the needs of a different one of the three markets described in question 4.

______________ The third company is offering one new product, which it is marketing exclusively to the market described in item C of question 4.

Product Development

6. Identify four common sources of ideas for new insurance products:

   1)______________________________

   2)______________________________

   3)______________________________

   4)______________________________

7. List the five steps involved in creating a product proposal:

   1)______________________________

   2)______________________________

   3)______________________________

   4)______________________________

   5)______________________________

8. Describe three of the activities carried out by members of various departments of an insurance company during the technical design stage of product development:

   1)______________________________

   ____

   2)______________________________

   ____

   3)______________________________

   ____

9. During the implementation stage of product development, the company obtains legal permission to sell the product, designs promotional and training materials, and initiates the systems and administrative activities necessary to support the product. What

are three activities that are carried out at this stage which involve promotional or training materials?

1) ____________________

____

2) ____________________

____

3) ____________________

____

10. Since test marketing of many insurance products is impractical, what method(s) might an insurer use instead of true test marketing?

____

____

11. Identify four of the factors that can be used to measure the success of a product.

1) ____________________

2) ____________________

3) ____________________

4) ____________________

The Role of the Agent

12. Identify some common sources that agents use to find prospects.

1) ____________________

2) ____________________

3) ____________________

13. Below are descriptions of several sales made by insurance agent Julia Bertram. By writing **S**, **T**, or **E** in the space provided, indicate whether each sale is an example of **single-need selling (S)**, **total-needs programming (T)**, or **estate planning (E)**.

____ Ms. Bertram sells a disability policy to a customer who has just moved to a new job that does not offer group disability coverage.

____ Ms. Bertram sells a second customer life insurance to pay taxes and legal fees related to the administration of the customer's affairs should the customer die.

____ Ms. Bertram sells a third customer life insurance to take care of all the customer's obligations in the event of the customer's death and to provide for the customer's family's various needs after the customer's death.

____ Ms. Bertram sells a fourth, young customer life insurance intended to pay back educational loans if the customer dies.

14. Name the authorities by whom a life insurance agent must be accredited in Canada and in the United States in order to sell investment-based life insurance products.

Canada______________________________

United States______________________________

15. Give the names of the sales practices, prohibited in most states and provinces, described below. Choose from the following: **misrepresentation, twisting, guaranteeing policy dividends**, and **rebating.**

______________ Suggesting that future dividends paid on a policy will equal or exceed a certain amount

______________ Persuading a customer to replace one policy with another without explaining all the differences between the two policies

______________ Offering to return a share of a policy's premium to a customer

______________ Making misleading statements about a policy that a customer is considering purchasing

16. Summarize three characteristics of well-written insurance business.

1)______________________________

____

2)______________________________

____

3)______________________________

____

17. Describe three alternatives to policy lapse that an agent might suggest to a policyowner who is unable to meet a current premium payment.

1) ______________________________

____

2) ______________________________

____

3) ______________________________

____

18. What are two of the primary service functions of an insurance agent and one type of periodic review that many agents conduct?

1) ______________________________

____

2) ______________________________

____

3) ______________________________

____

To assess your understanding of the material in this chapter, go to the Test Preparation Guide (TPG) for this course and work the sample questions from this chapter. The TPG will explain how to study for and take examinations and will provide you with practice in answering the types of questions that appear on FLMI examinations. Be sure to check your answers to see how well you have mastered the material covered in this chapter. If you have not mastered the material, then reread the chapter in the assigned textbook and rework the corresponding exercises in this student guide. Then return to the TPG and rework the sample questions provided.

Chapter 5

Agency-Building Distribution Systems

To help you prepare for the FLMI examination for this course, read the entire preface of this student guide. It contains many practical pointers that will help you in studying FLMI educational material. This student guide is designed to help you learn the material covered in the assigned textbook. Working the exercises in this student guide is not a substitute for reading the book. Be sure to read the assigned chapter in the book before completing the exercises in the corresponding chapter of the student guide. Consult the current LOMA Insurance Education Catalog for the correct text assignment for this course.

CHAPTER OVERVIEW

Once insurance companies have identified customers' insurance needs and created products to meet those needs, these companies must find a way to deliver products to the customers. In other words, they need a distribution system. Many companies in the life and health insurance industry distribute their products through agency-building distribution systems.

In this chapter, you read about three types of agency-building systems that life and health insurers use: the ordinary agency system, the multiple-line agency system, and the home service system. You learned about the two variations on the ordinary agency system -- the branch office system and the general agency system -- and the differences between them. You then learned about the three aspects of the operation of an agency: planning; implementing the plans, which involves recruiting, selecting, training, motivating, and supporting insurance agents; and controlling operations, which involves evaluating agency operations. You also saw how an insurance company's home office contributes to the running of its agencies. After that, you learned how the multiple-line agency system began and how it differs from the ordinary agency system. Finally, you were introduced to the home service system and the similarities and differences between it and the ordinary agency system.

After studying this chapter, you should be able to

- Describe the features of a personal selling distribution system
- Distinguish between the branch office system and the general agency system

- Explain several different ways of evaluating the performance of agents and an agency
- Describe some services that the home office marketing department performs to support agency operations
- Describe the different types of compensation paid to agents, general agents, and branch managers
- Describe the multiple-line agency system
- Explain the unique features of the home service distribution system

Outline of Major Topics Covered in this Chapter

I. Distribution Systems and the Personal Selling Distribution System
II. The Ordinary Agency System
    A. Introduction and Some Basic Definitions
    B. Types of Organization under the Ordinary Agency System
        1. Use of the branch office and general agency systems
        2. Branch office system
        3. General agency system
        4. Comparison of branch office and general agency systems
    C. Operation of the Ordinary Agency System
        1. Agency planning
            a. Factors affecting agency planning
            b. Operating budget
            c. Staffing schedule
        2. Implementing the agency's operating plan
            a. Importance of agents
            b. Recruiting new agents
            c. Agent training
            d. Agent motivation
            e. Providing administrative support
        3. Controlling agency operations
            a. Analyzing agent performance
            b. Analyzing agency performance
III. Agency Support
    A. Roles of Agency Services Unit and Human Resources Department
    B. Agent Training
    C. Agent Contracts and Licenses
        1. Contracts
        2. Licenses
            a. Types of licenses needed by insurance agents
            b. Home office licensing staff
    D. Compensation and Benefits
        1. Agent compensation
            a. Commissions
            b. Service fees
            c. Bonuses and benefits
            d. New-agent compensation
        2. Compensation for general agents and branch managers

E. Technical Support
F. Advertising and Sales Promotion
G. Office Services

IV. The Multiple-Line Agency (MLA) System

V. Home Service Distribution System
A. Products Sold by the Home Service System
B. Field Office Organization
C. Comparison of the Home Service System and the Ordinary Agency System
1. Similarities
2. Collecting and recording premiums
3. Transferring records
4. Compensating agents

Review of Key Terms and Concepts

Define the following key terms and concepts:

distribution system (p. 127)____

____

personal selling distribution system (p. 127)________________________

____

ordinary agency system (p. 128)_____________________________________

____

multiple-line agency (MLA) system (p. 128)__________________________

____

home service distribution system (p. 128)___________________________

____

career agent (p. 129)____

____

exclusive agent (p. 129)____

____

marketing territory (p. 129)____

____

branch manager (p. 130)____

____

general agent (p. 130)____

____

exclusive territory (p. 131)____

____

overlapping territory (p. 131)____

____

nonexclusive territory (p. 131)_______________________________________

____

operating budget (p. 135)____

____

staffing schedule (p. 135)____

____

aptitude test (p. 137)____

____

personality test (p. 137)____

____

interest test (p. 137)____

____

historical comparison (p. 142)____

____

intracompany comparison (p. 142)_____________________________________

____

intercompany comparison (p. 142)_____________________________________

____

expense ratio (p. 143)____

____

first-year commission (p. 148)____

____

renewal commission (p. 148)____

____

service fee (p. 149)____

____

vested renewal commission (p. 149)____

____

institutional advertising (p. 151)____

____

cross-selling (p. 153)____

____

debiting (p. 154)____

____

industrial life insurance (p. 154)____

____

combination company (p. 155)____

____

territory (p. 155)____

____

premium receipt book (p. 157)____

____

collection report (p. 158)____

____

WORKING OUTLINE

1. In the space provided below, write **O**, **M**, or **H** according to whether each statement describes the **ordinary agency system (O)**, the **multiple-line agency (MLA) system (M)**, or the **home service system (H)**.

   ____ Agents distribute industrial, or debit, insurance and collect premiums at the policyowner's home.

   ____ Agents distribute property/casualty insurance along with life and health insurance.

   ____ This system can be subdivided into the branch office system and the general agency system.

The Ordinary Agency System

2. Describe some of the tasks performed by a superintendent, or director, of agencies. The superintendent works with the home office to

   1)____

   ____

   2)____

   ____

   3)____

   ____

   and with district managers on such matters as

   1)____

   ____

   2)____

   ____

   3)____

   ____

3. Give the requested information concerning the branch office system and the general agency system in the categories indicated.

Branch office system

Personnel

Employed by: ______________________________

Under contract to: ______________________________

Receive commissions from: ______________________________

May they be transferred? __________

Branch manager

Spends how much time selling? ______________________________

Usual form of compensation: ______________________________

Expenses of the branch office

Usually paid by: ______________________________

General Agency System

General Agent

Spends how much time selling? ______________________________

May GA be transferred? __________

Usual form of compensation: ______________________________

____

Expenses of the general agency

Usually paid by: ______________________________

4. Mr. Anderson and Ms. Olafson are both general agents in Witherspoon County for the Alphabet Insurance Company. Witherspoon County has three sizable communities -- Statesville, Fayetteville, and Salem. Below are three descriptions of ways Witherspoon County could be divided into territories. For each description, indicate what type of territory -- **exclusive, overlapping,** or **nonexclusive** -- Mr. Anderson and Ms. Olafson would each be in charge of if the county were divided in the way described.

_______________ Only Ms. Olafson is authorized to represent Alphabet Insurance in Statesville and only Mr. Anderson is authorized to represent the company in Fayetteville, but they are both authorized to represent the company in Salem.

_______________ Only Ms. Olafson is authorized to represent Alphabet in Statesville and Salem, and only Mr. Anderson is authorized to represent the company in Fayetteville. The two general agents share no part of the county.

_______________ Both Ms. Olafson and Mr. Anderson are authorized to represent the company in the entire county.

5. Read the situations below. In each case, indicate whether the insurance company described would more likely choose to operate with the **general agency (GA) system** or the **branch office (BO) system.**

__________ Company P wants to be able to reward field personnel by promoting them to more lucrative territories when the personnel have performed well and also wants to be able to offer its personnel good opportunities for promotion within the company.

__________ Company Q wants there to be a close relationship between the costs of its agencies and their performance. The company can not afford to pay high payroll costs when agency production is low.

__________ Company R wants to have complete control over whether sales efforts will be increased or reduced in any particular territory at any particular time.

__________ Company S is a new company and does not wish to pay the full cost of establishing local offices.

* * *

Complete the following exercises concerning the operation of the ordinary agency system.

6a. Name the most important factor affecting a field office's operating plan and two other important factors.

Most important____

Secondary factor____

Secondary factor____

6b. Give the names of the parts of an agency's operating plan described below.

_______________ Predicts how many employees the agency will need and the costs of acquiring and maintaining them.

____________ Predicts the agency's level of business and also its expenses.

6c. ____ True or false? The best sources of prospective agents are established agents and agency managers.

6d. Identify below the types of tests that can be used to help select insurance agents.

____________ These tests identify a person's general interests.

____________ These tests identify a person's motivational, emotional, interpersonal, and attitudinal characteristics.

____________ These tests predict a person's ability to learn a specific job.

6e. Describe the type of information that LIMRA's Career Profile System gathers and the type of predictions it can be used to make.

____

____

____

____

6f. Identify some of the specific topics that fall into the following three broad areas which are often part of a comprehensive new agent training program.

Insurance basics______________________________

____

Sales and customer service techniques________________

____

Procedures__________________________________

____

6g. Identify the types of instructional techniques employed in the following two descriptions.

____________ The trainer pretends to be a customer and the trainee acts out a situation in which the trainee is selling the customer insurance.

________________ An experienced agent accompanies a new agent on a sales call.

6h. Identify two situations that could create the need for continuing agent training.

1)____

2)____

6i. What are some steps that agency managers and home office staff can take to motivate agents?

1)____

2)____

3)____

6j. What are some of the tasks that an agency's support staff perform to keep the agency running smoothly and to help agents?

To keep the office running smoothly:

1)____

2)____

3)____

To help the agents:

1)____

2)____

3)____

6k. In the table below, indicate with an **"X"** whether each of the factors listed that can be used to evaluate the performance of an insurance agent is a quantitative factor or a qualitative factor.

Factor	**Quantitative**	**Qualitative**
Product knowledge		
Personal organization		
Average premium per sale		
Dollar sales volume		
Attitude		

6l. Identify the types of comparison described below that can be used to evaluate and control agency operating expenses.

_______________ The performance of an agency is compared to those of other agencies in the same company.

_______________ The current performance of an agency is measured compared to its performance or the performance of other agencies in previous years.

_______________ The performance of an agency is compared to industry averages.

6m. If an agency's expenses are too low, the agency may incur an unacceptable level of indirect costs. What is meant by "indirect costs" in this situation?

____

____

____

____

6n. _____ True or false? The legal restrictions on agency operating costs specified in Section 4228 of the New York State Insurance Code apply to all business written by companies approved to do business in New York State, regardless of where the business is written.

6o. List three of the expense ratios frequently used to evaluate agency operating costs.

1)____

2)____

3)____

6p. Explain briefly what functional cost analysis is and what it can be used for.

____

____

____

____

*　　*　　*

Agency Support

Complete the exercises below concerning the types of services that insurance company home offices frequently provide to field offices.

7a. Describe two benefits of agent training provided by the home office over training provided through field offices.

1) ____

____

2) ____

____

7b. The contract between a soliciting agent and an insurance company usually contains a statement of the existence of the contract and a description of the authority of the agent to act for the company. Identify five other provisions usually found in an agent's contract.

1) ____

____

2) ____

____

3) ____

____

4) ____

____

5) ____

____

7c. Identify an additional provision usually found in a <u>general</u> agent's contract.

____

____

7d. Jane Joyner wishes to sell health insurance and investment-based life insurance in one jurisdiction. Name all the licenses and accreditations she needs to obtain, the courses she needs to take, and the examinations she must pass. Assume she wishes to work in a jurisdiction that has the maximum number of requirements.

1)____

2)____

3)____

4)____

5)____

7e. Under what circumstances would an agent obtain a temporary license?

____

____

7f. Give the names of the types of agent compensation described below. Choose from the following: **first-year commissions; renewal commissions; service (persistency) fees; bonuses; benefits; new-agent compensation.**

____________ A percentage of the annual premium rate, paid for a specified number of years after the policy's first year, generally to the person who sold the policy

____________ A percentage of the annual premium rate or a flat amount per $1,000 of insurance, paid every year that the policy is in force to the person who provides service to the policyowner

____________ Employer contributions to employee insurance and retirement plans

____________ Higher-than-usual commissions, monthly supplements, or advances against future earnings, paid to agents who are having trouble earning an adequate living

____________ Trips, merchandise, or cash given to reward production or persistency or both

____________ A percentage of the policy's initial premium, paid during the policy's first year

7g. Indicate in the spaces provided to the left of each statement whether the statement is true (**"T"**) or false (**"F"**).

____ Of general agents and branch managers, only branch managers typically receive a salary.

____ Only general agents receive overriding commissions.

7h. What types of situations does the advanced underwriting department usually become involved in and what support does it provide?

____

____

____

7i. Summarize the reasons that most insurance advertising is institutional advertising.

____

____

____

7j. What are typically some of the contributions of an insurance company's sales promotion unit?

____

____

7k. Besides providing company forms, stationery, rate books, and procedures manuals, what kinds of office services can an insurance company provide to its agencies?

____

____

____

* * *

The Multiple-Line Agency (MLA) System

8. Determine whether the following statements concerning the MLA system are true ("T") or false ("F").

____ One of the factors which led to the creation of the MLA system was the idea that life and health insurers could smooth their unpredictable profit and loss cycles by offering property/casualty insurance, which tends to have a more stable earnings pattern.

____ One drawback of cross-selling is that it increases the amount of prospecting necessary to generate new business.

____ One perceived advantage of cross-selling is that it improves persistency.

____ An advantage of the MLA system is that it allows companies and agents to benefit from economies of scale.

____ Most multiple-line career agents are considered employees of the insurance company rather than independent contractors, with the insurer establishing the agent's office and paying most of its expenses.

Home Service Distribution System

Answer the following questions concerning the home service distribution system.

9a. What is a debit? ______________________________

____

9b. What is the difference between the ordinary life products, such as monthly debit ordinary, distributed through the home service system and those distributed through the ordinary agency system?

____

____

9c. The home service system and the ordinary agency system differ in the areas of collecting and recording premiums, transferring records, and compensating agents. In summary, how does the home service system differ from the ordinary agency system in these areas?

Collecting and recording premiums

____

____

____

Transferring records

____

____

Compensating agents

____

To assess your understanding of the material in this chapter, go to the Test Preparation Guide (TPG) for this course and work the sample questions from this chapter. The TPG will explain how to study for and take examinations and will provide you with practice in answering the types of questions that appear on FLMI examinations. Be sure to check your answers to see how well you have mastered the material covered in this chapter. If you have not mastered the material, then reread the chapter in the assigned textbook and rework the corresponding exercises in this student guide. Then return to the TPG and rework the sample questions provided.

Chapter 6

Additional Distribution Systems

To help you prepare for the FLMI examination for this course, read the entire preface of this student guide. It contains many practical pointers that will help you in studying FLMI educational material. This student guide is designed to help you learn the material covered in the assigned textbook. Working the exercises in this student guide is not a substitute for reading the book. Be sure to read the assigned chapter in the book before completing the exercises in the corresponding chapter of the student guide. Consult the current LOMA Insurance Education Catalog for the correct text assignment for this course.

CHAPTER OVERVIEW

Some insurance companies distribute their products by other means than agency-building distribution systems. In this chapter, you read about some of these other distribution systems.

You learned about the brokerage system and the different ways insurance companies conduct their relations with agent-brokers. You learned what a personal producing general agent is and how the PPGA system works. You read that group insurance is more apt to be sold by salaried sales people than by commissioned sellers, and you learned about the process of selling group insurance. You also read about some other products that are sometimes sold by salaried sales people. You found out about the direct response distribution system and the different ways it can be implemented. Finally, you read about some characteristics of the location selling distribution system.

After studying this chapter, you should be able to

- Describe the features of distribution systems other than agency-building distribution systems
- Distinguish between an agent-broker, a career agent, and a personal producing general agent
- Explain why group insurance requires a method of distribution different from those used for individual products
- Describe the primary responsibilities of group representatives
- Name the types of products distributed through salaried sales personnel

- Describe the features of a direct response marketing campaign
- Explain how advertising effectiveness is tested
- Describe the features of a location selling distribution system

Outline of Major Topics Covered in this Chapter

I. Introduction to Additional Distribution Systems
II. Brokerage Distribution System
  A. Relationships between Insurance Companies and Brokers
  B. Soliciting Brokerage Business
  C. Compensation
  D. Home Office Support Services
III. Personal Producing General Agency (PPGA) Distribution System
  A. Relationships between Insurance Companies and PPGAs
  B. Compensation
  C. Differences between the PPGA System and the Brokerage System
IV. Salaried Sales -- Group Insurance
  A. Group Insurance and Group Representatives
  B. Prospecting
  C. Preparing the Proposal
  D. Installing the Product
    1. Informing group members about the product
    2. Enrollment of group members
  E. Negotiating Policy Renewals
  F. Home Office Support Services
V. Salaried Sales -- Other Products
  A. Pension Products
  B. Savings Bank Life Insurance (SBLI)
  C. Fraternal Life Insurance
VI. Direct Response Marketing
  A. Use of the Direct Response System
  B. Marketing Intelligence and Direct Response Distribution
    1. Direct response system use of marketing intelligence
    2. Target markets
  C. Designing Sales Promotion Materials
    1. Goals of direct response advertising
    2. Direct mail
    3. Print media
    4. Broadcast media
    5. Telemarketing
  D. Testing Advertising Effectiveness
VII. Location Selling Distribution System

Review of Key Terms and Concepts

Define the following key terms and concepts:

brokerage system (p. 161)______________________________

____

broker (pps. 161, 164)______________________________

____

personal producing general agency (PPGA) system (p. 161)______________

____

salaried sales distribution system (p. 162)______________________________

____

direct response distribution system (p. 162)______________________________

____

location selling distribution system (p. 162)______________________________

____

brokerage manager (p. 165)______________________________

____

brokerage shop (p. 165)______________________________

____

group representative (p. 169)______________________________

____

installation (p. 170)______________________________

____

noncontributory plan (p. 171)______________________________

____

contributory plan (p. 171)______________________________

____

direct response marketing (p. 173)______________________________

____

telemarketing (p. 173)____

____

guaranteed-issue (p. 175)____

____

direct mail (p. 177)____

____

mail kit (p. 177)____

____

print media advertising (p. 177)____________________________________

____

free-fall advertising (p. 177)______________________________________

____

broadcast media (p. 178)____

____

fulfillment kit (p. 178)____

____

WORKING OUTLINE

Brokerage Distribution System

1. Give two common reasons that agents sometimes choose to broker business.

   1)____

   ____

   2)____

   ____

2. Indicate whether the two insurers described below solicit brokerage business by means of a **brokerage manager** or a **brokerage shop.**

   ______________ The Brave Company gets its brokerage business through a general agent who is under contract to

____________ the Brave Company and to a number of other companies. He helps agent-brokers find insurance companies willing to insure customers that the agent-broker's own company has declined or rated.

____________ One of the Twin Company's employees is responsible for encouraging agent-brokers to sell the Twin Company's products.

3. An insurer typically does not pay an agent-broker the same commissions or service fees that it pays its own career agents nor does an insurer typically provide the agent-broker with the same training. Summarize the differences between the ways an insurer treats an agent-broker and a career agent in these matters.

   Commissions____

   ____

   Service fees_______________________________________

   ____

   Training____

   ____

Personal Producing General Agency (PPGA) System

4. In the spaces provided, give the information requested concerning the PPGA system. A PPGA

   engages primarily in__________________________________

   is usually under contract to______________________________

   is usually required to undergo training in

   ____

   is typically compensated with____________________________

   differs from a broker in that____________________________

   ____

Salaried Sales -- Group Insurance

5. Summarize three important characteristics of group insurance and the ways these characteristics affect distribution of group insurance products.

1) ____________________

____

____

____

2) ____________________

____

3) ____________________

____

____

* * *

In the following series of questions, give the information requested concerning the work of group representatives.

6a. Identify some important sources of prospects for group representatives.

____

____

____

6b. Identify some of the factors a group representative must take into account in preparing a proposal.

____

____

____

6c. Identify the types of information that an insurer and employer must convey to the group members during installation of a group plan.

1) ____________________

2) ____________________

3) ____________________

4) ____________________

5) ____________________

6d. For each of the following statements, indicate in the space in the left-hand column whether each statement is true (**"T"**) or false (**"F"**).

____ If a group plan is contributory, then group member enrollment is voluntary, but if the plan is noncontributory, then enrollment is automatic.

____ For most group policies, a group representative must design a new proposal every year.

____ Group representatives may work either in regional offices or in the company's home office.

* * *

Salaried Sales -- Other Products

7. Identify the different distribution methods used for the following insurance products:

Pension products____

____

SBLI____

____

Fraternal life insurance_________________________________

____

Direct Response Marketing

8. Give the information requested concerning insurance products commonly sold through direct response marketing.

Complexity____

____

Product design features__________________________________

____

Nature of coverage_______________________________________

____

Underwriting requirements________________________________

* * *

Complete the following exercises related to the activities involved in direct response marketing.

9a. What are some of the ways that insurance companies use marketing intelligence in direct response marketing?

9b. Complete the following sentence by circling the correct word/phrase in parentheses:

People who have purchased goods or services through direct response (are/are not) likely to continue to make such purchases.

9c. Explain why the following groups are common target markets for direct response insurance companies.

Credit card holders

Senior citizens

9d. Complete the following sentence by circling the correct words/phrases in parentheses:

(Like/Unlike) other insurance advertising, direct response advertisements (attempt/don't attempt) to induce customers to buy or seek information about a specific product immediately.

9e. What are some common sources of mailing lists?

9f. What is the main advantage of direct mail marketing?

____

____

9g. How does print media advertising compare to direct mail advertising according to the following criteria?

Audience reached____

____

Response rate and cost____

____

9h. Describe some of the characteristics of direct response radio and television advertisements.

____

____

9i. Telephone operators cannot usually accept orders for insurance products. What can they do instead?

____

9j. Name some benefits and a drawback of telemarketing as a tool for marketing insurance.

Benefit____

Benefit ____

Drawback____

9k. Identify three ways that advertisers can measure the effectiveness of their advertisements or proposed advertisements.

1)____

2)____

3)____

* * *

Location Selling Distribution System

10. What two steps can an insurer take to try to ensure that enough customers will be exposed to an insurance office for the office to be successful?

1) ____

2) ____

11. How much and what kind of prospecting do location-selling agents do?

____

____

To assess your understanding of the material in this chapter, go to the Test Preparation Guide (TPG) for this course and work the sample questions from this chapter. The TPG will explain how to study for and take examinations and will provide you with practice in answering the types of questions that appear on FLMI examinations. Be sure to check your answers to see how well you have mastered the material covered in this chapter. If you have not mastered the material, then reread the chapter in the assigned textbook and rework the corresponding exercises in this student guide. Then return to the TPG and rework the sample questions provided.

Chapter 7

Actuarial Functions for Individual Life Insurance

To help you prepare for the FLMI examination for this course, read the entire preface of this student guide. It contains many practical pointers that will help you in studying FLMI educational material. This student guide is designed to help you learn the material covered in the assigned textbook. Working the exercises in this student guide is not a substitute for reading the book. Be sure to read the assigned chapter in the book before completing the exercises in the corresponding chapter of the student guide. Consult the current LOMA Insurance Education Catalog for the correct text assignment for this course.

Chapter Overview

Much of the business of life and health insurance is based on mathematical calculations that are performed by actuaries. In this chapter, you learned about actuaries and their position within insurance companies. You read about the basic principles upon which their work is founded, and you were introduced to the types of work that they do in the area of individual life insurance.

You learned the principles behind the development of mortality rates and of the different types of mortality tables. You saw how net premiums are calculated. You learned how the calculation of gross premiums takes into account expenses, and you read about the types of expenses included in their calculation. You also read about the role of actuaries in the determination of policy reserves, cash values, and policy dividends. Finally, you learned about asset share calculations and the part actuaries play in product development.

After studying this chapter, you should be able to

- Describe the functions that actuaries perform
- List the responsibilities of the corporate actuarial unit
- Describe the factors that insurers consider when setting premium rates
- Give an example of the law of large numbers
- State the purpose of safety margins
- Distinguish between a select group and the general population

- Compare the effects of compound and simple interest

- Distinguish between net and gross premiums and explain how these premiums are calculated

- Describe the purpose of an asset share calculation

Outline of Major Topics Covered in this Chapter

I. Mathematics and Actuaries, and their Importance in Life and Health Insurance
II. What is an Actuary?
III. Actuarial Functions in an Insurance Company
  A. Actuarial Functions and Corporate Organizational Structure
  B. Actuarial Research
    1. Uses and sources of actuarial research
    2. Interest rates and income taxes
  C. Government Liaison
  D. Financial Statements and Reports
IV. Individual Life Insurance Calculations
V. Mortality Rates
  A. Probability and the Law of Large Numbers
  B. Calculating Mortality Rates
  C. Developing Mortality Tables
    1. What is a mortality table?
    2. A typical mortality table
    3. Adding safety margins
    4. Factors in developing mortality tables
    5. The selection process
  D. Individual Valuation Mortality Tables
    1. Valuation mortality tables and their use
    2. Ordinary life insurance valuation tables
    3. Individual annuity valuation mortality tables
VI. Interest and Interest Rates
  A. How Simple Interest and Compound Interest Work
  B. Present Value of Money
VII. Net Premiums
  A. How Net Premiums are Derived
  B. Net Single Premiums
  C. Net Level Annual Premiums
VIII. Gross Premiums
  A. Loading
  B. Operating Expenses
    1. Types of operating expenses
    2. Allocation of expenses
    3. Lapses
  C. Contingency Funds
  D. Profits and Contributions to Surplus
  E. Setting the Gross Premium
IX. Policy Reserves, Cash Values, and Policy Dividends
  A. Policy Reserves
  B. Cash Values

C. Policy Dividends
    1. Determining policy dividends
    2. Sources of surplus
    3. Dividend distribution

X. Product Development
  A. Actuaries, Product Development, and Corporate Organizational Structure
  B. Asset Share Calculations

Review of Key Terms and Concepts

Define the following key terms and concepts:

actuary (p. 181) ____________________

____

rate making (p. 186) ____________________

____

probability (p. 187) ____________________

____

law of large numbers (p. 187) ____________________

____

mortality curve (p. 188) ____________________

____

mortality table (p. 188) ____________________

____

basic mortality table (p. 191) ____________________

____

select group (p. 192) ____________________

____

select period (p. 193) ____________________

____

valuation mortality table (p. 193) ____________________

____

projection method (p. 195)

simple interest (p. 195)

compound interest (p. 195)

principal (p. 196)

discounting (p. 197)

present value (p. 197)

net premium (p. 197)

policy reserve (pp. 197, 206)

net single premium (p. 198)

level premium (p. 199)

loading (p. 200)

gross premium (p. 200)

lapse (p. 201)

lapse rate (p. 203)____

persistency rate (p. 203)__________________________________

profit (p. 205)____

contribution to surplus (p. 205)____________________________

cash value (p. 206)____

surplus (p. 207)____

divisible surplus (p. 207)__________________________________

asset share (p. 209)_______________________________________

asset share calculation (p. 209)____________________________

validation period (p. 211)__________________________________

validation point (p. 211)___________________________________

WORKING OUTLINE

1. Identify projects and duties for which actuaries use mathematics to make their calculations and predictions.

Now identify some of the trends that actuaries follow and research.

What is an Actuary?

2. Actuaries work with people in other departments to analyze certain aspects of insurance company operations. Give examples of company operations that are the concern both of actuaries and personnel in other company functional areas.

Actuarial Functions in an Insurance Company

3. Summarize some of the ways that actuaries use statistics gathered from throughout the company to influence the direction of the company's future strategies.

4. How do changes in interest rates and income tax laws affect the work of actuaries?

Interest rates

Income tax laws

5. Describe how actuaries interact with the government on matters affecting insurance companies.

____

____

____

6. Summarize the role of actuaries in the preparation of financial statements and reports for an insurance company.

____

____

____

____

Mortality Rates

7. To refresh your memory, restate the definition of mortality rate.

____

____

8. If you were to toss an unweighted coin 10 times, you might predict that the coin would come up "heads" on 50 percent of the tosses, but you probably wouldn't be too surprised if the coin turned up "heads" 70 percent or 30 percent of the time. On the other hand, if you tossed a coin ten million times, you ought to be very surprised if the number of tosses that resulted in a "head" were not extremely close to 50 percent.

   What is the name of the statistical concept described in the example above and how does the concept relate to life insurance?

____

____

____

____

* * *

Look at the 1980 CSO mortality table shown in your textbook (page 190). Answers to the questions below appear at the end of this chapter.

9a. What is the mortality rate for 55-year-old men? ________________

9b. Out of 100,000 55-year-old men, then, how many can be expected to die during the course of a given year?

____

9c. What is the mortality rate for 27-year-old women? ______________

* * *

The following series of questions applies to adding safety margins to mortality tables.

10a. How does an insurer add a safety margin to a life insurance mortality table?

____

____

10b. Why would the insurer add a safety margin to a life insurance mortality table?

____

____

10c. What would an insurer do differently when adding a safety margin to an **annuity** mortality table as opposed to an **insurance** mortality table? Why?

____

____

10d. What is the name for a mortality table without a safety margin, and what do actuaries use such tables for?

____

____

* * *

11. Three groups of people presently 45 years old can be described as follows:

Group	Status
X	Insured at standard rates 10 years ago
Y	Insured at standard rates 3 years ago

Z Insured at standard rates within the last year

Arrange the three groups (X, Y, and Z) in order from the group with the lowest mortality rate to the group with the highest mortality rate. (Answers appear at the end of the chapter.)

Lowest mortality rate -------------------> Highest mortality rate

Group ______ Group ______ Group ______

* * *

Answer the following questions about valuation mortality tables.

12a. What type of margins of safety do valuation mortality tables usually have?

____

12b. What is the current valuation table used in the United States to calculate life insurance reserves?

____

12c. What tables are used in Canada to calculate life insurance reserves?

1)______________ 3)______________

2)______________

12d. What is the most commonly used annuity mortality table?

____

12e. Instead of developing new mortality tables, actuaries frequently assume that mortality will improve by set percentages each year. What is the name of this method of updating mortality tables and what is the rationale behind using it?

____

____

____

* * *

Interest and Interest Rates

13. Assume you invest $1,000 today at 10 percent interest. Indicate

below, using simple interest and compound interest, how much interest you would earn (a) after one year and (b) after two years. (Use the space below for calculations and to show your answers. Correct answers are provided at the end of this chapter.)

(a) Simple interest after one year | Compound interest after one year

(b) Simple interest after two years | Compound interest after two years

Net Premiums

The following series of questions concerns net premiums.

14a. Net premiums are derived from combining what two factors?

________________________ and ________________________

14b. In each of the following sentences, circle the word(s) in parentheses that correctly complete each sentence.

A conservative table, such as the 1980 CSO table, shows (higher/lower) mortality rates than some other tables and, therefore, results in (higher/lower) net premiums.

High interest rates (raise/lower) net premiums.

The net premiums used to calculate policy reserves are based on conservative assumptions -- (high/low) mortality rates and (high/low) interest rates.

The premium rate that is charged to the policyowner is usually based on (more/less) conservative assumptions than those the policy reserves are based on.

14c. What is involved in pricing policies retrospectively and prospectively, and for what types of products do actuaries use each method?

____

____

____

14d. Identify which of the following descriptions is of a **net single premium** and which is of a **net level annual premium.**

______________ The amount of money that must be collected at the time a block of policies is issued to assure the accumulation of enough money to pay the death benefits on the policies.

______________ The amount of money that must be collected from living policyowners at the beginning of each policy year in order to pay all expected claims on a block of policies.

14e. Circle the words in the parentheses that correctly complete the following sentence.

With net level annual premiums, policyowners pay (more/less) in premiums during the early years of the contract than is necessary to pay for death benefits during those years and pay (more/less) in premiums during the latter years of the contract than is necessary to pay for death benefits during those years.

* * *

Gross Premiums

15. Apart from interest and mortality rates, what factor does a gross premium take into account? ______________________________

16. What does the loading portion of a gross premium pay for?

1)____

2)____

3)____

4)____

17. Explain or give examples of the types of insurance company expenses that fall into the following categories.

Development expenses____

____

Acquisition expenses____

____

Distribution expenses____

____

Maintenance expenses____

____

Termination expenses____

____

General administrative expenses

____

____

18. Of a block of 1,000 policies, 85 lapse before their second annual premium is paid.

What is the lapse rate of this block of policies? _____________%.

What is the persistency rate of this block of policies?

___________%. (Answers shown at the end of the chapter.)

19. In each of the following four pairs of possible circumstances, circle the one factor on each line that is more likely to lead to a lower lapse rate.

1. Premiums are paid monthly	Premiums are paid annually
2. Premiums are paid by EFT	Premiums are paid by mail
3. The insured is 25 years old	The insured is 55 years old
4. The policyowner has a high income	The policyowner has a low income

20. Why do actuaries create contingency funds?

____

____

Policy Reserves, Cash Values, and Policy Dividends

21. One function that actuaries perform is calculating policy reserves, which are amounts of money that insurance companies set aside. What do they set aside these amounts for?

____

____

____

22. Another actuarial task is to calculate the cash values of in-force policies. What is the source of a policy's cash value?

____

____

____

23. Actuaries must also decide how much of a company's premiums received to return to policyowners in the form of dividends. What two decisions must be made after determining the amount of a company's surplus for a year in order to decide the nature and size of the company's dividends?

1)______________________________

____

2)______________________________

____

24. If a company's actual results differ from its projected results, its surplus can be affected. A company's surplus can be affected by any difference between a company's actual and assumed levels of

1)______________ 3)______________

2)______________

25. Indicate some of the factors actuaries might consider in arriving at their calculation of the company's divisible surplus.

____

Product Development

26. What does an asset share calculation show?

27. What can an actuary do if the results of an asset share calculation are not satisfactory?

28. Why are asset share calculations for some of the more recently developed types of life insurance policies particularly challenging?

29. Besides asset share calculations, summarize some of the other work that actuaries perform as part of product development.

ANSWERS TO SELECTED QUESTIONS

9a. 10.47 per 1,000

9b. 1,047

9c. 1.22 per 1,000

11. Z, Y, X

13.

	SIMPLE	**COMPOUND**
(a)	1,000 x.10 ----- **$100 (after 1st year)**	1,000 x.10 ----- **$100 (after 1st year)**
(b)	1,000 x.10 ----- $100 (2nd year) + 100 (1st year) ----- **$200 (after 2 years)**	1,100 (1,000 + 100) x.10 ----- $110 (2nd year) + 100 (1st year) ----- **$210 (after 2 years)**

18. lapse rate = .085

persistency rate = .915

To assess your understanding of the material in this chapter, go to the Test Preparation Guide (TPG) for this course and work the sample questions from this chapter. The TPG will explain how to study for and take examinations and will provide you with practice in answering the types of questions that appear on FLMI examinations. Be sure to check your answers to see how well you have mastered the material covered in this chapter. If you have not mastered the material, then reread the chapter in the assigned textbook and rework the corresponding exercises in this student guide. Then return to the TPG and rework the sample questions provided.

Chapter 8

Actuarial Functions for Group and Health Insurance

To help you prepare for the FLMI examination for this course, read the entire preface of this student guide. It contains many practical pointers that will help you in studying FLMI educational material. This student guide is designed to help you learn the material covered in the assigned textbook. Working the exercises in this student guide is not a substitute for reading the book. Be sure to read the assigned chapter in the book before completing the exercises in the corresponding chapter of the student guide. Consult the current LOMA Insurance Education Catalog for the correct text assignment for this course.

CHAPTER OVERVIEW

The work that actuaries do in the areas of group insurance and health insurance both resembles and differs from the work actuaries do for individual life insurance. In this chapter, you learned about these similarities and differences.

You learned the five main activities of a group insurance actuary. You read about some types of mortality tables used for group insurance, as well as about rate-making techniques used for group insurance. You saw how group insurance premiums are calculated. You also learned about the factors that affect the size of an experience rating refund, and about the purpose of claim fluctuation reserves.

You learned about the statistics that are needed to develop health insurance products, the method that is used to calculate health insurance premiums, and some of the morbidity tables that are used to calculate health insurance reserves.

After studying this chapter, you should be able to

- Describe the role of experience rating in group insurance
- Distinguish between manual rates and blended rates
- Show how gross premiums are computed and how the monthly gross premium for a group is calculated
- Describe the factors that determine a group's experience rating refund

- Distinguish between morbidity tables and mortality tables

- Recognize the basic formula for calculating annual claim costs for individual health insurance

Outline of Major Topics Covered in this Chapter

I. Functions of a Group Insurance Actuary
II. Group Life Insurance
    A. Features of Group Life Insurance
    B. Mortality Tables
    C. Premiums
        1. Experience rating, manual rates, and blended rates
        2. Minimum initial gross premiums
        3. Calculating group premiums
        4. Experience rating refunds
            a. Claim experience
            b. Group size
            c. Expenses incurred
    D. Claim Fluctuation Reserve
III. Health Insurance
    A. Disability Income Insurance and Medical Expense Insurance
    B. Morbidity Statistics
        1. Types of statistics required
        2. Continuance tables
    C. Premiums
        1. Individual health insurance
        2. Group health insurance
    D. Reserves
        1. Individual health insurance
        2. Group health insurance

Review of Key Terms and Concepts

Define the following key terms and concepts:

master contract (p. 215)____

____

experience rating (p. 217)______________________________________

____

manual rates (p. 217)____

____

blended rates (p. 217)____

____

dividend (p. 219)____________________

experience rating refund (p. 219)____________________

claim fluctuation reserve (p. 221)____________________

disability income insurance (p. 221)____________________

medical expense insurance (p. 221)____________________

morbidity rate (p. 222)____________________

aggregate claims (p. 222)____________________

claim frequency rate (p. 222)____________________

continuance table (p. 223)____________________

annual claim costs (p. 224)____________________

WORKING OUTLINE

Functions of a Group Insurance Actuary

1. Describe the five main actuarial activities involved in developing **group** insurance plans.

   1)____________________

   2)____________________

   3)____________________

4) ______________________________

5) ______________________________

Group Life Insurance

* * *

The following series of questions applies to the actuarial function and group life insurance.

2a. What type of group constitutes about 90 percent of the groups insured by group insurance? ______________________________

2b. In this type of group, who is the policyholder and who are the persons insured? ______________________________

2c. About 99 percent of group life insurance is what type of insurance?

____

2d. Compare the factors considered in setting premiums for one-year term group life insurance with the factors considered in setting premiums for individual whole life insurance.

____

____

____

____

2e. Identify and describe some mortality tables that are frequently used for group life insurance.

____

____

____

____

* * *

3. Identify whether **experience rating, manual rates,** or **blended rates** are being used in each of the group life insurance premium calculation situations described on the next page.

_______________ The Alpha Company's premium is based on the mortality experience of an average group.

_______________ The Beta Company's premium is based entirely on the group's prior claim experience.

_______________ The Omega Company's premium is based partly on the group's prior experience and partly on the experience of an average group.

Of **experience rating, manual rates,** or **blended rates,** which would most likely be used in determining group life premiums for the following groups?

_______________ A large group -- more than 1,000 members

_______________ A medium-sized group

_______________ A very small group

* * *

The following series of questions applies to the actuarial function at the Greenleaf Life Insurance Company.

4a. Greenleaf Life is calculating a renewal premium for one of its United States group life insurance policyholders. The client has decided to provide $20,000 of insurance for each of its employees. Greenleaf Life has calculated a monthly premium rate per $1,000 of $0.25, based on the attained age of the the group members insured at the time of the calculation of the premium, the predicted administrative expenses associated with the policy, and some consideration of the claim experience of the group.

If 50 employees are covered at the beginning of the year, the amount of the client's first monthly premium can be calculated as follows:

Total amount of insurance per employee (in thousands)	$20
x total number of employees	50

= total amount of insurance (in thousands)	$1,000
x average monthly premium rate per $1,000 of insurance	$0.25

= total monthly premium	$ 250

During the first month, two employees leave the company and four others join the company. Calculate the client's premium for the second month of the contract. (Answers appear at the end of the chapter.)

Total amount of insurance per employee (in thousands) _____

x total number of employees _____

= total amount of insurance (in thousands) _____

x average monthly premium rate per $1,000 of insurance

= total monthly premium _____

4b. Name some factors -- aside from number of employees -- that would affect the client's monthly premium amount.

1) ______________________________

2) ______________________________

3) ______________________________

4c. In all likelihood, how long will Greenleaf guarantee this premium rate?

____

4d. At roughly the same time that it is calculating the client's new premiums, Greenleaf is deciding whether to return any part of the previous year's premiums to the client. Because the client's policy is nonparticipating, this refund is called a(n)

______________________________.

4e. Determine whether the following factors should be expected to **increase** or **decrease** the likelihood that the client will receive a refund.

__________ The group incurred fewer claims than Greenleaf had predicted.

__________ Greenleaf considers this group to be a relatively small group.

__________ Greenleaf's expenses for the year were lower than expected.

4f. Greenleaf will use a part of the excess premium resulting from the client's favorable claim experience to fund a claim fluctuation reserve. Explain the reason for establishing this reserve.

____

____

____

Health Insurance

* * *

The following questions deal with the factors involved in calculating health insurance premiums.

5a. Distinguish between morbidity rates and mortality rates.

____

____

5b. What three figures are multiplied in order to determine the amount of a company's aggregate claims?

____

x ______________________________

x ______________________________

5c. What are some of the factors that must be forecast in order to determine average claim cost?

____

____

____

5d. Continuance tables are one tool that might be used to help determine average claim cost. Give an example of the type of information that might be contained in a continuance table for medical expense insurance and in a continuance table for disability income insurance.

Medical expense insurance______________________________

____

____

Disability income insurance______________________________________

____

____

* * *

6. Assume that a group of actuaries has predicted that, for a block of 1,000 major medical policies covering 45-year-old men, there will be 60 claims averaging $1,200 per claim. Calculate the annual claim costs for this block of policies and the net one-year premium. (Answers are shown at the end of the chapter.)

Expected number of claims	______
x average amount payable per claim	$______
= annual claim costs	$______
÷ number of insureds	______
= net one-year premium	$______

What would the actuaries add to this net premium in order to arrive at a gross premium?

____

7. Identify and describe some of the morbidity tables that actuaries use to calculate reserves for health insurance.

____

____

____

____

ANSWERS TO SELECTED QUESTIONS

4a.

Total amount of insurance per employee (in thousands)	$ 20
x total number of employees	52
= total amount of insurance (in thousands)	$1,040
x average monthly premium rate per $1,000 of insurance	$ 0.25
= **total monthly premium**	**$ 260**

6.

Expected number of claims	60
x average amount payable per claim	$ 1,200
= annual claim costs	$72,000
÷ number of insureds	1,000
= **net one-year premium**	**$ 72**

To assess your understanding of the material in this chapter, go to the Test Preparation Guide (TPG) for this course and work the sample questions from this chapter. The TPG will explain how to study for and take examinations and will provide you with practice in answering the types of questions that appear on FLMI examinations. Be sure to check your answers to see how well you have mastered the material covered in this chapter. If you have not mastered the material, then reread the chapter in the assigned textbook and rework the corresponding exercises in this student guide. Then return to the TPG and rework the sample questions provided.

Chapter 9

The Underwriting Function

To help you prepare for the FLMI examination for this course, read the entire preface of this student guide. It contains many practical pointers that will help you in studying FLMI educational material. This student guide is designed to help you learn the material covered in the assigned textbook. Working the exercises in this student guide is not a substitute for reading the book. Be sure to read the assigned chapter in the book before completing the exercises in the corresponding chapter of the student guide. Consult the current LOMA Insurance Education Catalog for the correct text assignment for this course.

CHAPTER OVERVIEW

The process of assessing the amount of risk presented by applicants for insurance is called underwriting. In this chapter, you learned about what the underwriting function involves in a life and health insurance company.

First, you learned about the goals of underwriting and about the different types and levels of underwriters. Then you learned about the first steps of the underwriting process. You read about the sources of information that underwriters have aside from the application and the agent. After that, you became familiar with the factors that can cause an applicant to be considered a greater-than-average life insurance risk. You went on to learn about how life insurance underwriters classify applicants into risk classes, and how the underwriters then assign premium rates to the applicants.

Health insurance underwriting was the focus of the next section of the chapter. You learned about some of the different ways that health insurance underwriters can deal with greater-than-average risks. Next, you read about the underwriting characteristics specific to group insurance. You then were introduced to reinsurance, the different types of reinsurance treaties, and the different reinsurance plans. You finished up by reading a summary of the types of interactions that underwriters have with other insurance company personnel.

After studying this chapter, you should be able to

- Describe the underwriting process and its purpose
- List and explain the major objectives of the underwriter

- Explain the role of agents in risk selection
- Identify a variety of sources of underwriting information
- Discuss risk factors that influence the underwriting decision
- Describe the risk classes used by life insurance underwriters
- Explain how the numerical rating system is used
- Explain the different risk factors used in health insurance underwriting and life insurance underwriting
- Contrast the underwriting of group insurance with the underwriting of individual insurance
- Explain the purpose of reinsurance and describe different reinsurance treaties and plans

Outline of Major Topics Covered in this Chapter

I. What is Underwriting?
II. The Underwriting Decision
    A. Equitable to the Client
    B. Deliverable by the Agent
    C. Profitable to the Company
III. The Underwriting Function
IV. The Underwriting Process
    A. Field Underwriting
    B. Application Processing and Preliminary Review
        1. Initial processing
        2. Jet screening
        3. Computer screening
V. Additional Information Sources for Risk Selection
    A. Attending Physician's Statement (APS)
    B. Medical Information Bureau (MIB)
    C. Inspection Reports and Telephone Interviews
VI. Risk Factors for Life Insurance
    A. Introduction
    B. Medical Risk Factors
        1. Weight
        2. Physical condition other than weight
        3. Family health history
        4. Smoking
    C. Nonmedical Risk Factors
        1. Occupation
        2. Aviation
        3. Avocation or hobbies
        4. Substance abuse
        5. Moral hazard
        6. Foreign residence or travel

        7. Insurable interest
        8. Antiselection
        9. Finances

VII. Risk Classification for Life Insurance
    A. Risk Classes
    B. Underwriting Manuals
    C. The Numerical Rating System
        1. How the system works
        2. Assigning numerical values to risk factors
        3. Risk classes and the numerical rating system
    D. Premiums for Substandard Risks
        1. Increasing, constant, and decreasing underwriting hazards
        2. Extra-percentage tables
        3. Flat extra premiums
        4. Reducing substandard premium rates

VIII. Underwriting Individual Health Insurance
    A. Assessing Risk Factors for Health Insurance
        1. Comparison to assessment of life insurance risk factors
        2. Occupation
        3. Antiselection
        4. Moral hazard
        5. Finances
    B. Rating Substandard Risks in Health Insurance

IX. Underwriting Group Life and Health Insurance
    A. Comparison to Individual Insurance Underwriting
    B. New Business
        1. Sources and uses of information
        2. Nature of the group
        3. Age distribution of the members
        4. Level of participation
        5. Benefits
        6. Occupational hazards
        7. Size of the group
    C. Renewals

X. Reinsurance
    A. Participants in and Reasons for Reinsurance
    B. Retention Limits
    C. Reinsurance Treaties
        1. Automatic reinsurance treaty
        2. Facultative reinsurance treaty
            a. Facultative-obligatory (fac-ob) reinsurance treaty
    D. Reinsurance Plans
        1. Proportional and nonproportional plans
        2. Yearly renewable term (YRT)
        3. Coinsurance
        4. Modified coinsurance (modco)
        5. Stop-loss and catastrophic reinsurance plans

XI. Relationships with Other Company Personnel
    A. Sales and Marketing
    B. Actuaries
    C. Policy Issue
    D. Customer Service
    E. Claim Administration

Review of Key Terms and Concepts

Define the following key terms and concepts:

underwriting (p. 228)____________________

rating an application (p. 232)____________________

field underwriting (p. 233)____________________

worksheet (p. 234)____________________

jet screening (p. 236)____________________

computer screening (p. 236)____________________

Attending Physician's Statement (APS) (p. 237)____________________

Medical Information Bureau (MIB) (p. 238)____________________

inspection report (p. 239)____________________

underwriting impairment (p. 239)____________________

substance abuse (p. 243)____________________

insurable interest (p. 244)____________________

antiselection (p. 244) ______________________________

____

risk class (p. 245) ______________________________

____

underwriting manual (p. 246) ______________________________

____

numerical rating system (p. 249) ______________________________

____

credit (p. 249) ______________________________

____

debit (p. 249) ______________________________

____

extra-percentage tables (p. 251) ______________________________

____

net amount at risk (p. 252) **A policy's death benefit minus that policy's reserve at the end of the policy year.***

flat extra premium (p. 252) ______________________________

____

accident risk (p. 255) ______________________________

____

illness risk (p. 255) ______________________________

____

pre-existing condition provision (p. 255) ______________________________

____

impairment rider (p. 256) ______________________________

____

*Please note that the definition given above is the *correct* definition for ***net amount at risk.*** The first printing of *Operations of Life and Health Insurance Companies,* Second Edition, incorrectly defines ***net amount at risk.*** Please check your copy of the text. If the definition of ***net amount at risk*** in your text does not match the correct definition entered for you above, please change it.

good distribution of risk (p. 257)______________________________

____

reinsurance (p. 260)______________________________

____

ceding company (p. 260)______________________________

____

reinsurer (p. 260)______________________________

____

retention limit (p. 261)______________________________

____

retrocession (p. 261)______________________________

____

retrocessionaire (p. 261)______________________________

____

reinsurance treaty (p. 262)______________________________

____

automatic reinsurance treaty (p. 263)______________________________

____

automatic binding limit (p. 263)______________________________

____

facultative reinsurance treaty (p. 263)______________________________

____

facultative-obligatory (fac-ob) reinsurance treaty (p. 264)______________________________

____

proportional reinsurance (p. 264)______________________________

____

nonproportional reinsurance (p. 264)____________________

yearly renewable term (YRT) plan (p. 265)________________

coinsurance (p. 265)____________________________

modified coinsurance (modco) plan (p. 266)________________

stop-loss reinsurance plan (p. 266)____________________

catastrophic reinsurance plan (p. 266)__________________

WORKING OUTLINE

The Underwriting Decision

1. An underwriter's goal is to approve and issue a policy that is equitable to the client, deliverable by the agent, and profitable to the company. Explain what is required to satisfy these objectives.

   Equitable to the client

   Deliverable by the agent

Profitable to the company

____

____

____

The Underwriting Function

2. As the experience and authority of an underwriter increase, what is the underwriter usually given greater authority to do?

____

____

Summarize some of the tasks fulfilled by physicians and nurses who are employed by insurance companies.

____

____

____

The Underwriting Process

*   *   *

In the following series of questions, provide the required information about field underwriting.

3a. What are agents trained to verify concerning an applicant's completion of an insurance application?

____

3b. Identify four of the types of information that agents should seek if an applicant mentions health problems on an application.

1)____

2)____

3)____

4)____

3c. What are agents expected to do if the answers to any of the questions on an application seem unusual?

____

3d. What kind of information does an agent report in an agent's statement?

____

____

* * *

4. Summarize some of the information that is verified and reviewed during a preliminary review of a life insurance application.

____

____

____

____

5. ____ True or false? Jet unit personnel are typically authorized to rate or decline applications for insurance.

6. State briefly some characteristics of insurance applications that are suitable for jet screening.

1)____

2)____

3)____

4)____

5)____

Additional Information Sources for Risk Selection

7. Determine whether the following statements are true or false. Write **"T"** or **"F"** in the space provided.

____ An Attending Physician's Statement is usually a quick way to obtain underwriting information but generally contains relatively little information of value.

____ Insurance companies request information from the Medical Information Bureau (MIB) in order to check for evidence of risk factors that the proposed insured has failed to mention in an application for insurance.

____ Insurance companies must gain the written consent of the person being investigated in order to obtain information from the MIB, and they cannot base underwriting decisions solely on information provided by the MIB.

____ Only certain authorized insurance company personnel have access to MIB information, and they are responsible for updating MIB information if they find any inaccuracies.

____ Insurers have the right to initiate inspection reports without informing the proposed insureds.

____ Rather than ordering inspection reports, insurance companies frequently have members of their underwriting staff gather information by telephoning the proposed insured directly, if the amount of insurance sought is not too high.

Risk Factors for Life Insurance

8. The descriptions in the right-hand column below are of people who are subject to one of the following medical or nonmedical life insurance underwriting risk factors:

- physical condition other than weight
- family health history
- moral hazard
- insurable interest
- antiselection
- finances

Identify in the space provided which of these risk factors to which each person is subject.

______________ A policyowner, who might otherwise have considered letting a policy lapse, keeps the policy in force because the insured's health has deteriorated.

______________ A proposed insured suffers from high blood pressure.

______________ A proposed insured has previously been convicted of a felony.

______________ A proposed insured seems to be applying for an amount of insurance for which the premiums would be more than the proposed insured can afford to pay.

____________ Several members of a proposed insured's family have died from or presently suffer from diabetes.

____________ A person is applying for insurance on the life of another person, but it doesn't seem that the applicant would suffer any financial loss if the proposed insured were to die uninsured.

List additional medical and nonmedical life insurance risk factors that insurers consider.

Medical

1)________________________

2)________________________

Nonmedical

1)________________________

2)________________________

3)________________________

4)________________________

5)________________________

Risk Classification for Life Insurance

9. Identify the common name of the life insurance risk class into which each of the following groups of people would be classified.

____________ People who represent an average mortality risk

____________ People whose risk of early death is so great that the company won't insure them at any premium rate

____________ People who represent a higher-than-average risk and who the company will insure at a higher premium rate than that charged to average risks

____________ People who represent a lower-than-average risk

____________ People who have not smoked for 12 months before applying for insurance

10. What information is commonly found in an underwriting manual?

____

____

____

____

11. Assume that the Penultimate Life Insurance Company uses the numerical rating system for underwriting individual life insurance applications and that an average risk receives a rating of 100. Indicate what the applicant's numerical rating would be in each of the following situations. (Answers appear at the end of the chapter.)

a. ____________ Proposed insured A's application indicates a favorable factor worth 20 points.

b. ____________ Proposed insured B's medical examination reveals an unfavorable factor worth 30 points.

c. ____________ Underwriters assign proposed insured C a debit of 45 points.

d. ____________ Underwriters assign proposed insured D a credit of 10 points.

e. ____________ Applicant E is assigned a debit of 30 points for poor family health history, a debit of 15 points for high blood pressure, and a credit of 10 points for being a nonsmoker.

12. In the following table, put an **"X"** in the appropriate space in order to indicate whether each description is of the extra-percentage tables method of computing premiums for substandard risks or of the flat extra premium method.

	Extra-percentage tables	**Flat extra premium**
A specific additional premium amount is assessed for each $1,000 of insurance. The additional amount does not vary with the age of the insured.		
Risks are divided into broad classes, according to their numerical ratings, and extra premiums are calculated for the average extra mortality expected for each class.		

	Extra-percentage tables	Flat extra premium
This premium computation method is useful when the extra risk is constant or temporary.		
This premium computation method is useful when the extra risk increases with the age of the insured.		

13. In what situation would an insurer consider reducing a substandard premium rate?

____

____

In what type of situation would an insurer impose a probationary period on reduction of a substandard premium rate and what would this procedure entail?

____

____

____

____

Underwriting Individual Health Insurance

14. Why is insurable interest usually not as much of a concern for health insurance underwriters as it is for life insurance underwriters?

____

15. Identify some occupations that belong in the following health insurance risk classifications.

Least hazardous ______________________________

Hazardous ______________________________

Most hazardous ______________________________

Uninsurable ______________________________

16. Explain why health insurance underwriters are particularly concerned with the following risk factors.

Antiselection

____

____

Moral hazard

____

____

Finances

____

____

17. What are three ways that health insurance underwriters can modify insurance coverage?

1)____

2)____

3)____

Underwriting Group Life and Health Insurance

18. Any large group of people includes individuals who would be substandard or uninsurable risks if they were evaluated for insurance on an individual basis. Considering this fact, how is it that insurers avoid paying unacceptable amounts in group insurance claims?

____

____

19. Explain what requirements a group needs to fulfill in order to meet group underwriting standards. The requirements are related to the following general categories.

The nature of the group

____

____

The age distribution of the group members

____

____

The level of participation

____

____

____

Benefits

____

____

Occupational hazards

____

____

Size of the group

____

____

____

20. When evaluating an insured group for renewal of a contributory plan, on what two factors do underwriters focus?

    1)____

    2)____

Reinsurance

21. Generally, what are the two reasons that insurance companies reinsure their business?

    1)____

    ____

2) ____________________

____

____

22. What company personnel are commonly in charge of an insurance company's reinsurance operations?

____

____

____

23. Why do insurance companies set retention limits?

____

____

24. What are some of the factors that insurers consider when setting retention limits?

1) ____________________

2) ____________________

3) ____________________

25. In reinsurance terms, what does it mean to "recapture" business?

____

____

26. Identify some ways that a ceding company can benefit from the experience and expertise of a reinsurer's underwriters.

____

____

____

____

27. Identify the types of reinsurance treaties described below.

____________ The ceding company sends a copy of each application to the reinsurer, who makes an independent underwriting decision on every risk.

_______________ The ceding company cedes all eligible policies which exceed its retention limit, and the reinsurer accepts every amount ceded up to its automatic binding limit.

_______________ The ceding company cedes only selected risks, and the reinsurer accepts every risk ceded.

28. Discuss the benefits and drawbacks either to the ceding company or the reinsurer of each type of reinsurance treaty. Also indicate the situations in which each type of reinsurance treaty would commonly be used.

Automatic treaty

____

____

____

Facultative treaty

____

____

____

Fac-ob treaty

____

____

____

* * *

Give the information requested concerning the different types of reinsurance plans.

29a. **Yearly renewable term (YRT)**

Is it proportional or nonproportional reinsurance?

____

What does the ceding company purchase from the reinsurer?

____

____

What is the amount of reinsurance coverage?

___

___

For what is the reinsurer liable and not liable?

___

___

Does YRT have a premium refund provision? ___

Two benefits of the YRT plan:

1)___

2)___

29b. **Coinsurance**

Is it proportional or nonproportional reinsurance?

___

* * *

Assume ceding company A -- which has a retention limit of $50,000 -- issues a policy for $200,000 and cedes $150,000 to reinsurer B. Under these circumstances, the reinsurer is entitled to 75 percent of

___

and is liable for 75 percent of

___.

If this policy is terminated voluntarily, reinsurer B is liable for ___

* * *

An important benefit of a coinsurance plan is that

___

One drawback of a coinsurance plan is that

___

____

____

29c. **Modified coinsurance (modco)**

Is it proportional or nonproportional reinsurance?

____

In a modco plan, the reinsurer receives its share of ____________ minus an allowance for ______________________________.

All reserves for a policy reinsured under a modified coinsurance plan are held by ______________________________.

What does the reinsurer do at the end of each year relative to the company's reserves?

____

29d. **Stop-loss reinsurance**

Is it proportional or nonproportional reinsurance?

____

Create an example of a basic stop-loss reinsurance plan agreement:

____

____

____

29e. **Catastrophic**

Is it proportional or nonproportional reinsurance?

____

Under what circumstances is the reinsurer liable? ______________

____

____

Under a catastrophic plan, the reinsurer pays ________________; the reinsurer's liability is limited to ______________________

____.

Relationships with Other Company Personnel

Summarize the types of contact that underwriters have with the following insurance company personnel.

30a. **Sales and Marketing**

30b. **Actuaries**

30c. **Policy Issue**

30d. **Customer Service**

30e. **Claim Administration**

ANSWERS TO SELECTED QUESTIONS

11a. 80

11b. 130

11c. 145

11d. 90

11e. 135

To assess your understanding of the material in this chapter, go to the Test Preparation Guide (TPG) for this course and work the sample questions from this chapter. The TPG will explain how to study for and take examinations and will provide you with practice in answering the types of questions that appear on FLMI examinations. Be sure to check your answers to see how well you have mastered the material covered in this chapter. If you have not mastered the material, then reread the chapter in the assigned textbook and rework the corresponding exercises in this student guide. Then return to the TPG and rework the sample questions provided.

Chapter 10

The Customer Service Function

To help you prepare for the FLMI examination for this course, read the entire preface of this student guide. It contains many practical pointers that will help you in studying FLMI educational material. This student guide is designed to help you learn the material covered in the assigned textbook. Working the exercises in this student guide is not a substitute for reading the book. Be sure to read the assigned chapter in the book before completing the exercises in the corresponding chapter of the student guide. Consult the current LOMA Insurance Education Catalog for the correct text assignment for this course.

CHAPTER OVERVIEW

Without customer satisfaction and a positive image among agents and prospective insureds, an insurance company cannot keep its business in force nor can it successfully market its products. The customer service function is vital to an insurance company's growth and even its survival.

Chapter 10 described the broad range of activities that constitute the customer service function. You learned about the different ways that insurance companies organize customer service activities. You also read in detail about typical customer service activities for both individual and group insurance products.

After studying this chapter, you should be able to

- List several types of customers that insurance companies serve
- Describe some skills needed by employees who provide effective customer service
- Discuss different ways to organize the customer service function in a company
- Describe customer service functions that must be performed for individual and group insurance

Outline of Major Topics Covered in this Chapter

I. Who Is the Customer?
  A. External Customer and Internal Customers

B. Policyowners
C. Agents
D. Beneficiaries
E. Account Holders

II. Who Provides Customer Service?
A. Skills Needed by Customer Service Representatives

III. Organization of Customer Service Departments
A. Functional Organization
B. Product Organization
C. Customer Organization
D. Geographical Organization
E. Team Organization

IV. Customer Service for Individual Life Insurance
A. Changing Policy Coverage
1. Policy conversions
2. Supplementary benefit riders
3. Reissues
a. Reducing the death benefit
b. Changing insureds
4. Reinstatements
B. Policy Values
1. Policy loans
2. Premium loans
3. Policy dividends
4. Surrenders
C. Replacements
1. 1035 exchanges
2. Policy updates
D. Noncoverage Changes
1. Name and address changes
2. Beneficiary changes
3. Ownership changes
E. Recordkeeping
1. Insurance program updates

V. Customer Service for Group Insurance
A. Opening a New Group Insurance Account
1. Establishing policyholder service records
2. Processing enrollments
B. Maintaining Policy Records
C. Terminating Group Coverage

Review of Key Terms and Concepts

Define the following key terms and concepts:

customer service (p. 271)____

____

external customer (p. 272)_______________________________________

____

internal customer (p. 272) ______________________________

____

conversion privilege (p. 284) ______________________________

____

rider (p. 285) ______________________________

____

supplementary benefit rider (p. 285) ______________________________

____

irrevocable beneficiary (p. 288) ______________________________

____

minimum deposit business (p. 289) ______________________________

____

replacement (p. 290) ______________________________

____

endorsement (p. 293) ______________________________

____

preferred beneficiary (p. 293) ______________________________

____

recording method (p. 294) ______________________________

____

endorsement method (p. 294) ______________________________

____

absolute assignment (p. 294) ______________________________

____

collateral assignment (p. 294) ______________________________

____

WORKING OUTLINE

1. When does the customer service relationship between an insurance company and its customers begin? How long does this relationship last?

____

____

Who Is the Customer?

An insurance company's customers can be divided into two general categories -- external customers and internal customers.

2. Give some examples of external customers.

(1)__________________ (2)__________________

(3)__________________ (4)__________________

3. Give some examples of internal customers.

(1)__________________ (2)__________________

(3)__________________ (4)__________________

4. Name some insurance company customers that are both internal customers and external customers.

____

____

5. Mildred Fenton purchased an insurance policy from the Bayside Life Insurance Company. What activities might Ms. Fenton ask Bayside's customer service area to perform in relation to her insurance policy?

____

____

6. An insurance company's customer service area can help the company's insurance agents in many ways. What types of policyowner questions might an agent refer to the customer service area?

____

____

7. How can customer service representatives help agents to obtain sales leads and to conserve business?

____

____

8. What types of questions should a customer service representative expect from a beneficiary after an insured has died?

____

____

____

____

9. ____ True or False? Before the death of the insured, an irrevocable beneficiary is entitled to only basic policy information.

Who Provides Customer Service?

10. ____ True or False? Customer service representatives are the only insurance employees who are called upon to provide customer service.

11. Suzanne McFadden has recently been hired by the Tabular Life Insurance Company as a customer service representative. Tabular is one of an increasing number of insurance companies who expect their customer service representatives to provide sophisticated service in addition to traditional administrative assistance. Tabular gives Ms. McFadden authority to make customer decisions and expects her to come up with creative solutions to customers' problems. Tabular also wants Ms. McFadden to develop skills and knowledge beyond its traditional expectations for customer service representatives. Briefly give examples of how the following skills will help Ms. McFadden perform her job successfully.

Communication skills____

____

Broad interpersonal skills___________________________________

____

Understanding of customers' motivations________________________

____

Computer skills____

____

Knowledge of company products________________________________

____

Knowledge of the company's position relative to the industry_____

____

Organization of Customer Service Departments

12. The most common organizational structures for customer service departments are functional organization, product organization, customer organization, or geographical organization. The descriptions below apply to these different types of organizational structure. In the space next to each description, write **"F"** if the structure is functional, **"P"** if the structure is by product, **"C"** if the structure is by customer, or **"G"** if the structure is geographical. Each letter may appropriately be used once, more than once, or not at all.

____ Each customer service representative performs one task or a few tasks that are similar in nature.

____ Each customer service representative must be highly skilled in all aspects of customer service.

____ The times that customer service representatives begin their work day can be scheduled to reflect the time zones that each representatives' specific customers live in.

____ A company establishes three customer service units: one services group life customers, one services group health customers, and one services individual life customers

____ This structure is popular with agents and policyowners, because they know exactly who in the company to contact for customer service.

____ This structure can be particularly useful in a company that markets investment-based products.

____ One drawback to this structure is that a customer who has more than one policy with a company must deal with more than one customer service representative.

13. ____ True or False? Different types of organizational structures are never used in combination with one another.

14. List three responsibilities that are unique to customer service specialists who deal with investment-based products.

(1)____

(2)____

(3)____

15. A number of insurance companies use the team structure for the customer service area. Indicate whether each of the following statements regarding the team structure form of organization is true or false by writing **"T"** or **"F"** next to each statement.

____ Each team serves a particular region or group of customers.

____ Within the team, each member is trained for only a specified customer service function.

____ The team plans its own work and vacation schedules, and even addresses disciplinary matters within the team.

____ The team organization functions best with a relatively small customer base and small staff.

Customer Service for Individual Life Insurance

16. Identify some of the most common administrative functions performed by customer service personnel.

____

____

____

____

17. What five steps must a customer service representative follow before a conversion can be processed?

(1)____

(2)____

(3)____

(4)____

(5)____

18. ____ True or False? Once a conversion is approved, a new policy is issued to replace the old one.

____ True or False? Payment of the first premium is always required at the time a policy conversion is requested.

19. Indicate which of the following factors a customer service representative would typically consider when evaluating a request for a supplementary benefit rider by placing an **"X"** in the space beside each such factor.

____ The type and amount of coverage

____ The type of supplementary benefit rider and amount of coverage requested

____ The amount of time remaining in the policy's suicide period

____ The risk classification of the insured

____ The insured's family health history

____ The length of time the present policy has been in force

____ The amount of time since the last evidence of insurability was submitted

20. Circle the words in parentheses that correctly complete the following sentence:

A request for a supplementary benefit rider is often approved immediately if the risk factors are (more/less) favorable and if the requested amount is (large/small).

21. Why is canceling a rider easier than adding one?

____

____

22. What are two situations in which a policyowner might want to have an insurance policy reissued?

____

____

23. Circle the word that correctly completes the following sentence:

When a policyowner decides that he or she is (overinsured/underinsured), the policyowner may request a reduction in the death benefit of his or her current policy.

In reducing the death benefit on an existing policy, what three activities does a customer service representative usually perform?

(1)________________________________

(2)________________________________

(3)________________________________

24. Describe a situation in which it would be desirable (and possible) to transfer an insurance policy's coverage from one insured to another.

____

____

25. Indicate whether the following statements about reinstatement are true or false by writing a **"T"** or an **"F"** in the space beside each statement.

____ The policyowner must send a signed request for reinstatement to the insurer within a specified period after the policy has lapsed.

____ The policyowner need not pay policy premiums that came due during the period of lapse, but must begin paying current premiums once a reinstatement has been approved.

____ Any policy loan that was outstanding at the time of policy lapse may be forgiven or it may be restored.

____ The longer the period of policy lapse, the more likely that the insurer will require evidence of insurability upon reinstatement.

____ The smaller the amount of coverage, the more likely that the insurer will require evidence of insurability upon reinstatement.

26. Reinstatement of a lapsed policy would be **more** advantageous to a policyowner than purchase of a new policy if

(1)________________________________

(2)________________________________

(3)________________________________

Reinstatement of a lapsed policy would be **less** advantageous to a policyowner than purchase of a new policy if

____

27. One of the most common inquiries a customer service department receives involves a policy's financial values. Cite four specific questions a policyowner might ask about his or her policy's financial values.

(1)____

(2)____

(3)____

(4)____

28. When a policyowner requests a policy loan, why is it important for the customer service specialist to know whether the policy has been assigned and whether an irrevocable beneficiary has been named?

____

____

29. What does an insurance company typically do if a policyowner requests a loan for an amount greater than the policy's loan value?

____

30. What are the benefits to an insurer of premium payments made by automatic premium loan?

____

____

31. ____ True or False? A policyowner is usually allowed to change the dividend option at any time during the lifetime of the policy.

____ True or False? Evidence of insurability is not required for any type of dividend option change.

32. Briefly describe the responsibilities of the customer service function with regard to policy dividends.

____

____

33. When a customer service representative receives a policyowner's request for the cash surrender of the policy, what action will the representative take with respect to

assignment of policy ownership?____________________

conservation?____________________

34. Describe four customer service functions associated with replacements.

(1)____________________

(2)____________________

(3)____________________

(4)____________________

35. When a policy is replaced, how does the use of a 1035 exchange benefit both the insurer and the policyowner?

____

____

36. When the customer service staff receives a request to make a noncoverage change in a policy, the customer service representative must first ascertain that the requester is identified as a person with the right to request the change and must make sure that the policy has not been assigned to another person.

____ True or False? Address changes require substantiating evidence, as do name changes.

____ True or False? The policyowner's signature is required on a request for a beneficiary change.

____ True or False? The present beneficiary's signature is required for a beneficiary change, whether the present beneficiary has been designated revocably or irrevocably, or else the change cannot be made.

37. Marie Hawkins, a policyowner from Calgary, Alberta, purchased a life insurance policy that was issued on June 8, 1961. She wants to make a beneficiary change and designate a preferred beneficiary for this policy. Indicate by writing a **"P"** in the appropriate space which of the following people are part of the preferred beneficiary class.

____ Ms. Hawkins' husband

____ Ms. Hawkins' supervisor at work

____ Ms. Hawkins' children

____ Ms. Hawkins' nephew

38. Identify two ways in which an insurer might allow a beneficiary change by the endorsement method.

(1) ______________________________

(2) ______________________________

39. Circle the word(s) that correctly complete the following sentence:

An insurer (will/will not) be bound by an absolute assignment if the policyowner has not notified the insurer in writing that the assignment has been made.

40. Joseph Wynn, a resident of a community property state, purchased an insurance policy on his life and named his wife Susan as revocable beneficiary. Joseph and Susan had been married for several years when he purchased the policy. If Joseph and Susan later divorce, what claim, if any, will Susan have on the policy? Discuss briefly.

____

____

____

41. Explain the responsibilities of a customer service staff in conjunction with a transfer of ownership of a split-dollar plan.

____

____

____

42. The customer service specialists at the Nuance Life Insurance Company are required to maintain and store records and policy documents on a timely basis. Identify three groups that may conduct audits of Nuance's records.

(1) ______________ (2) ______________

(3) ______________

43. State and provincial regulators require that any complaints that Nuance receives in the course of its business must be recorded. What specific information about complaints is Nuance required by regulators to keep?

____

____

Cite three benefits that Nuance can realize from studying its records of complaints.

(1)____

(2)____

(3)____

Customer Service for Group Insurance

44. When administering new group insurance accounts, customer service representatives establish policyholder service records. They must also perform two other functions. Name and describe them.

____

____

45. Identify four kinds of information contained in a group's policy file.

(1) ____________________________ (2)____________________________

(3) ____________________________ (4)____________________________

46. Each member of the group insurance plan must complete an enrollment card that identifies the beneficiary and gives the insurer demographic information about the group member.

____ True or False? The Jumbo Toy Company group insurance plan is self-administered; therefore, its enrollment cards are maintained by the insurance company's customer service department.

47. Place an **"X"** in the space beside each function that an insurer's customer service staff would normally perform in administering a group insurance plan.

____ Record additions to and deletions from coverage

____ Record premiums received

____ Record claims, commissions, and other payments

____ Send billing statements and notify the policyholder and the group representative when premium payments are overdue

____ Handle complaints from the policyholder and individual group members

48. Briefly describe the responsibilities of the insurer's customer service staff upon termination of a group insurance contract, with respect to conversions of the members' insurance coverage.

____

____

To assess your understanding of the material in this chapter, go to the Test Preparation Guide (TPG) for this course and work the sample questions from this chapter. The TPG will explain how to study for and take examinations and will provide you with practice in answering the types of questions that appear on FLMI examinations. Be sure to check your answers to see how well you have mastered the material covered in this chapter. If you have not mastered the material, then reread the chapter in the assigned textbook and rework the corresponding exercises in this student guide. Then return to the TPG and rework the sample questions provided.

Chapter 11

Claim Administration

To help you prepare for the FLMI examination for this course, read the entire preface of this student guide. It contains many practical pointers that will help you in studying FLMI educational material. This student guide is designed to help you learn the material covered in the assigned textbook. Working the exercises in this student guide is not a substitute for reading the book. Be sure to read the assigned chapter in the book before completing the exercises in the corresponding chapter of the student guide. Consult the current LOMA Insurance Education Catalog for the correct text assignment for this course.

CHAPTER OVERVIEW

An insurance company's claim area is important to the insurer's image because the claim area carries out the insurer's financial promises with its customers. Claim personnel must deal with claimants promptly, correctly, and with good human relations skills.

In Chapter 11, you read about typical organizational structures of claim areas. You learned about claim procedures, and you followed the claim investigation and decision process step-by-step for life insurance, medical expense insurance, and disability insurance.

After studying this chapter, you should be able to

- Describe several different ways in which the claim area can be organized
- Outline the basic steps involved in the claim decision process
- Discuss the types of information available to claim examiners during the investigation of an insured's death
- Give some reasons why insurance companies might deny individual life insurance claims
- List and describe six features of medical expense claims that are not normally found in life insurance claims

- Distinguish between the factors involved in processing medical expense claims and those in processing disability income claims

- Explain the concepts of coordination of benefits and deductible amounts

Outline of Major Topics Covered in this Chapter

I. Structure of the Claim Function
II. The Claim Decision Process
    A. Verifying Policy Status
    B. Verifying Coverage of the Insured
    C. Examining for Misrepresentation
    D. Verifying the Loss
    E. Determining the Amount of Benefits
    F. Determining the Recipients of Benefits
III. Investigating Claims
    A. Features of Claim Investigation
    B. Documenting a Claim Investigation
IV. Life Insurance Claim Procedures
    A. Acceptable Proofs of Death
    B. Paying a Life Claim
    C. Denying a Life Claim
V. Health Insurance Claim Procedures
    A. Medical Expense Insurance Claims
        1. Exclusions
        2. Waiting periods
        3. Pre-existing conditions
        4. Deductibles
        5. Coinsurance
        6. Coordination of benefits
    B. Processing Medical Expense Claims
    C. Disability Income Insurance Claims
        1. Processing and investigating disability claims
        2. Making a disability claim decision
        3. Vocational rehabilitation programs

Review of Key Terms and Concepts

Define the following key terms and concepts:

claim examiner (p. 299)____

____

claimant (p. 299)____

____

fraudulent claim (p. 303) ______________________________

____

rescission (p. 304) ______________________________

____

contestable period (p. 304) ______________________________

____

claim form (p. 304) ______________________________

____

claim investigation (p. 306) ______________________________

____

hearsay evidence (p. 308) ______________________________

____

interpleader (p. 311) ______________________________

____

waiting period (p. 314) ______________________________

____

pre-existing condition (p. 315) ______________________________

____

pre-existing conditions provision (p. 315) ______________________________

____

deductible (p. 315) ______________________________

____

per cause deductible (p. 315) ______________________________

____

calendar year deductible (p. 315) ______________________________

____

coinsurance (p. 316)____

____

stop-loss provision (p. 316)____

____

coordination of benefits (COB) clause (p. 316)______________________

____

total disability (p. 320)____

____

partial disability (p. 320)____

____

residual benefit for partial disability (p. 320)____________________

____

vocational rehabilitation (p. 322)__________________________________

____

WORKING OUTLINE

Structure of the Claim Function

1. ____ True or False? The larger the insurance company and the greater the variety of products the company sells, the less likely that the claim function is organized into separate claim units for each type of product.

   ____ True or False? Insurers who wish to provide quick, personal claim service to customers in a particular geographical area can do so effectively with a regional claim office structure.

2. Horace Bateman, the supervising claim examiner in a regional claim office of the Municipal Life Insurance Company, is authorized to process routine life insurance claims of up to $100,000 and group life insurance claims of up to $250,000 without home office approval. Mr. Bateman is also authorized to approve health and disability claims up to specified dollar limits. What would Mr. Bateman's likely response be if he receives a claim for an amount above his approval limits?

   ____

3. ____ True or False? The authority and responsibility of a claim examiner is directly related to the sizes and types of claims the examiner can approve.

The Claim Decision Process

4. Claim examiners follow a basic claim decision process, regardless of the type of coverage, amount of the claim, or individual situation. What seven questions must be satisfactorily answered before a claim can be approved?

(1)______________________________

(2)______________________________

(3)______________________________

(4)______________________________

(5)______________________________

(6)______________________________

(7)______________________________

5. ____ True or False? Verifying that a policy was in force when a loss occurred is time-consuming because many records must be looked through manually.

6. Briefly describe two situations in which a claim might be submitted under a policy for a person who is not covered by the policy. Include one example of fraud and one example of an honest mistake.

Fraud______________________________

Honest mistake______________________________

____

7. Claims that are submitted during a policy's contestable period are routinely scrutinized to guard against the possibility that the policy application contained falsified information. Factors that influence insurability and that may be falsified on an application include information about the insured's

(1) ______________________________

(2) ______________________________

(3) ______________________________

8. Once a claim examiner has determined that a particular claim is to be paid, the examiner must calculate the amount of the insurer's liability. In the following list, place an **"X"** beside the factors that the claim examiner must consider in calculating the benefit amount to be paid:

____ any premiums paid in advance

____ deductibles

____ coinsurance

____ any interest payments

9. Describe two situations in which life insurance policy proceeds cannot be distributed exactly as the policyowner has requested.

(1)____

(2)____

When may medical expense and disability benefits be payable to someone other than the insured person?

____

Investigating Claims

10. ____ True or False? The majority of life insurance claims require extensive investigation.

____ True or False? Of the life claims that need investigation, most require the hiring of field investigators or outside professional agencies to conduct the investigation.

____ True or False? A life insurance claim indicating that an insured's death might have been caused by accident or suicide is likely to require extra investigation.

11. The extent of a life insurance claim investigation is determined by a number of factors. In the following list, place an **"X"** alongside the factors that influence the extent of a claim investigation.

____ The insured's age

____ The amount of the insurer's potential liability

____ The circumstances surrounding the loss

____ The place where the loss occurred

____ The organizational structure of the company's claim area

____ The cause of the loss

____ The beneficiary who is making the claim

____ The provisions of the policy

12. A claim investigation requires information-gathering from one or a number of sources. Identify three sources a claim examiner might use during life insurance claim investigations.

    (1) ____

    (2) ____

    (3) ____

13. Briefly discuss how concern for an individual's right to privacy affects claim investigations.

    ____

    ____

    ____

14. Why should claim investigations be carefully documented?__________

    ____

15. ____ True or False? Hearsay evidence and an investigator's personal opinions can appear in a claim file as long as they are well-documented.

Life Insurance Claim Procedures

16. What are acceptable proofs of death in the United States and Canada?

    United States________________________________

    ____

    Canada____________________________________

    ____

17. Place **"Y"** for yes and **"N"** for no alongside each of the following situations to indicate whether an insurer's claim staff would be

likely to require an Attending Physician's Statement and/or an autopsy report when processing a claim for life insurance benefits.

____ Walter Carver died of cancer six months after he purchased an insurance policy on his life.

____ Hazel Wong, whose policy contained accidental death benefits, died when she fell from an open window.

____ Jennelle Carrero died of a heart attack seven years after she purchased an insurance policy on her life.

____ Henri Ferrer died mysteriously one year after his policy went into effect.

18. ____ True or False? When life insurance policy proceeds are payable to an insured's estate or to a minor child, additional documentation may be required to support the claimant's right to be paid.

19. Give four reasons that an insurer might deny a claim for life insurance benefits.

(1) ______________________________

(2) ______________________________

(3) ______________________________

(4) ______________________________

20. From the following list, place an "X" beside the methods a claimant and an insured can use to resolve a dispute over the denial of an individual life insurance claim.

____ litigation

____ negotiation

____ compromise settlement

21. When there are conflicting claimants to a life insurance policy's benefits, in what way are insurers in the jurisdictions listed below allowed to transfer the funds to a third party until the dispute is settled?

United States ______________________________

Quebec ______________________________

Other Canadian provinces ______________________________

Health Insurance Claim Procedures

22. The risk an insurer incurs for health insurance is different from that incurred for life insurance in that the health insurance benefit can vary widely, whereas the life insurance benefit is basically specified in the policy. Identify some factors that determine the amount of benefit payable under a health insurance policy.

____

____

____

23. List six specific features of medical expense insurance coverage that are not characteristic of life insurance coverage.

(1) ____________________ (2) ____________________

(3) ____________________ (4) ____________________

(5) ____________________ (6) ____________________

24. Place an **"E"** alongside each of the following conditions or treatments that would be excluded from coverage in most medical expense insurance contracts.

____ Sarah Linebarger undergoes a surgical facelift in order to look younger.

____ Marty Prinz has surgical repair of a superficial head wound that was caused by a failed suicide attempt.

____ George Lazzarro undergoes surgery to remove a tumor that existed prior to his becoming insured and that is specifically identified in an exclusionary endorsement to the policy.

____ Margaret Thomason undergoes plastic surgery to repair injuries to her face that resulted from an automobile accident.

25. ____ True or False? The typical 14- to 30-day waiting period following policy issue applies to medical expenses arising from accidents, but not sickness.

____ True or False? Waiting periods of three to six months are established for certain conditions such as appendicitis and tonsillitis.

26. ____ True or False? The pre-existing condition provision on group long-term disability coverage is intended to protect the insurer from the expense of underwriting every member of the group.

27. Mel Hite had an appendectomy and a surgical removal of his gallbladder in the same year, in two separate operations. The deductible amount Mr. Hite would pay under his medical expense insurance policy depends on the type of deductible his policy contains. Determine which type of deductible would result in each payment amount. Assume that there is a $100 deductible. In the blank next to each description, write **"CY"** for calendar year deductible or **"PC"** for per cause deductible.

____ A deductible amount of $100 for the appendectomy and a deductible amount of $100 for the gallbladder surgery.

____ A total deductible amount of $100 for both operations.

* * *

The following questions apply to Joe DeWitt's major medical insurance policy.

28a. Joe DeWitt's policy provides a $100 per cause deductible feature and a 20 percent coinsurance feature. How much would he be required to pay on medical claims for each of the following amounts? (Answers shown at the end of the chapter.)

(1) $1,100?____________________

(2) $3,000?____________________

28b. Under what circumstances would a stop-loss provision come into effect on Joe DeWitt's policy?

____

____

____

* * *

29. When a person is said to be overinsured, what does this mean? Why is overinsurance discouraged?

____

____

30. Company A is Julia Knobb's primary group medical expense insurer and Company B is her secondary medical expense insurance plan. What must occur before Company B will pay any benefits for Ms. Knobb?

____

____

31. Identify four types of professional consultants that an insurance company might employ on a full- or part-time basis to assist claim examiners with nonroutine claim decisions.

(1) ____________________ (2) ____________________

(3) ____________________ (4) ____________________

32. Why is it important for claimants to submit originals of medical receipts rather than copies?

____

____

33. Disability income claims are usually more difficult to process than medical expense claims? Why?

____

____

34. What is the purpose of limiting the amount of disability income insurance that may be purchased to a percentage of the individual's earned income?

____

____

35. ____ True or False? The waiting period (elimination period) for disability income insurance is the same as the waiting period for medical expense insurance.

36. Briefly discuss the elimination period for disability income insurance, as to its

typical length______________________________________

purpose ______________________________________

37. How does the definition of total disability in policies issued today differ from its definition in most older disability income policies?

____

____

38. ____ True or False? Determining whether a person is unable to work because of a disability is difficult, because a condition that is disabling to one person may not disable another person.

39. Once a claim examiner has received a disability claimant's statement with its accompanying physician's report, it is sometimes necessary for the examiner to contact the claimant, the attending physician, and, in cases of group insurance, the claimant's employer. Briefly describe the information the examiner would be likely to seek from

the claimant____

____

the attending physician____________________________________

____

the employer____

____

40. ____ True or False? The claim staff's decision as to whether a disability claimant is totally disabled is based solely on the opinion of the attending physician.

41. Give two reasons that insurers in the United States hesitate to conduct surveillance in disability cases in which fraud is suspected.

(1)____

(2)____

42. Circle the words/phrases that correctly complete the following passage:

Disability claims are most commonly (approved/denied). Some claims are settled -- that is, only a portion is approved. A typical settlement calls for (periodic payments/a lump sum payment) to the disabled claimant.

43. Describe four ways that vocational rehabilitation can help disabled persons again find gainful employment.

(1) ______________________________

(2) ______________________________

(3) ______________________________

(4) ______________________________

ANSWERS TO SELECTED QUESTIONS

28a. **(1) $300**

$100 deductible + $200 copayment [(1,100 - 100) x .20]

(2) $680

$100 deductible + $580 copayment [(3,000 - 100) x .20]

To assess your understanding of the material in this chapter, go to the Test Preparation Guide (TPG) for this course and work the sample questions from this chapter. The TPG will explain how to study for and take examinations and will provide you with practice in answering the types of questions that appear on FLMI examinations. Be sure to check your answers to see how well you have mastered the material covered in this chapter. If you have not mastered the material, then reread the chapter in the assigned textbook and rework the corresponding exercises in this student guide. Then return to the TPG and rework the sample questions provided.

Chapter 12

The Investment Function

To help you prepare for the FLMI examination for this course, read the entire preface of this student guide. It contains many practical pointers that will help you in studying FLMI educational material. This student guide is designed to help you learn the material covered in the assigned textbook. Working the exercises in this student guide is not a substitute for reading the book. Be sure to read the assigned chapter in the book before completing the exercises in the corresponding chapter of the student guide. Consult the current LOMA Insurance Education Catalog for the correct text assignment for this course.

CHAPTER OVERVIEW

The investments made by life and health insurance companies help to fuel economic growth in almost every aspect of the economy in the United States and Canada. Investments made by insurance companies also benefit policyowners and beneficiaries; in addition, investments help support the company's operations.

In Chapter 12, you read about typical structures and operations of the investment function, factors that affect life and health insurers' investment policies, and the types of investments that insurers make.

After studying this chapter, you should be able to

- Explain why an insurance company's investments are important both to that company's operations and to society
- Describe different ways insurers can organize their investment function
- Explain the purpose of asset-liability matching and some methods of accomplishing this matching
- Describe the procedure for setting and implementing investment policy
- Explain the factors that insurance company investment analysts consider in choosing investments

- Distinguish between stocks and bonds, and between different types of stocks and bonds

- Describe investments other than stocks and bonds that are part of an insurer's investment portfolio

Outline of Major Topics Covered in this Chapter

I. Investments, Society, and Insurance Company Operations
II. Organizational Structure of the Investment Function
    A. Departmental Structure
    B. Asset Management Structure
    C. Independent Investment Companies
III. Setting Investment Policy
    A. Policies Set by the Investment Committee
    B. Operational Planning
IV. Types of Investments
    A. Stocks
        1. Common stock
        2. Preferred stock
        3. Stock investment operations
    B. Bonds
        1. Bond investment operations
        2. Information about bonds
    C. Mortgages
        1. Mortgage operations
            a. Acquisition through mortgage correspondents
            b. Mortgage-backed securities
    D. Real Estate
        1. Restrictions on real estate purchases
        2. Reasons to invest in real estate
        3. Methods of acquiring real estate
V. Relationships with Other Departments

Review of Key Terms and Concepts

Define the following key terms and concepts:

portfolio (p. 328)____

____

asset-liability matching (p. 330)____________________________

____

segmentation of accounts (p. 331)____________________________

____

spin-off (p. 332) ______________________________

____

rate of return (p. 334) ______________________________

____

diversification (p. 334) ______________________________

____

liquidity (p. 334) ______________________________

____

stocks (p. 336) ______________________________

____

equity (p. 337) ______________________________

____

common stock (p. 337) ______________________________

____

prudent investor rule (p. 337) ______________________________

____

preferred stock (p. 339) ______________________________

____

participating preferred stock (p. 339) ______________________________

____

cumulative preferred stock (p. 339) ______________________________

____

convertible preferred stock (p. 339) ______________________________

____

floating rate preferred stock (p. 339) ______________________________

____

stock market (p. 340) ____________________

____

stock exchange (p. 340) ____________________

____

bond (p. 341) ____________________

____

bond certificate (p. 341) ____________________

____

maturity date (p. 341) ____________________

____

callable bond (p. 342) ____________________

____

convertible bond (p. 342) ____________________

____

prior claim (p. 342) ____________________

____

municipal bond (p. 342) ____________________

____

general obligation bond (p. 342) ____________________

____

revenue bond (p. 344) ____________________

____

corporate bond (p. 344) ____________________

____

secured bond (p. 344) ____________________

____

debenture (p. 344) ____________________

____

public offering (p. 344) ____________________

____

private placement (p. 344) ____________________

____

bond yield (p. 345) ____________________

____

bond rating (p. 345) ____________________

____

default (p. 346) ____________________

____

mortgage (p. 346) ____________________

____

amortized loan (p. 346) ____________________

____

escrow account (p. 347) ____________________

____

adjustable-rate mortgage (ARM) (p. 348) ____________________

____

mortgage correspondent (p. 349) ____________________

____

pass-through certificate (p. 349) ____________________

____

collateralized mortgage obligation (CMO) (p. 349) ____________________

____

sale-and-leaseback transaction (p. 352)________________________________

____

lessee (p. 352)____

____

net lease (p. 352)____

____

WORKING OUTLINE

1. What effects can the investments of insurance companies have on society?

   ____

   ____

2. Describe how the performance of an insurer's investments can affect the prices that company charges for its products.

   ____

   ____

Organizational Structure of the Investment Function

3. In one common form of investment department structure, four portfolio managers report directly to the vice president. Typically, each portfolio manager is responsible for administering a group of investments in one of these four areas, which reflect the most common investments held by insurers:

   (1) ____________________ (2)____________________

   (3) ____________________ (4)____________________

4. The Promotion Life Insurance Company has recently restructured its investment department by dividing it into two parallel units, one for making pension fund investments and one for making insurance-related investments. Place an "A" beside each advantage that Promotion is likely to achieve in this new organizational structure:

   ___ Clear lines of accountability ___ A small and efficient staff

   ___ Clear lines of control ___ No duplication of tasks

5. Write **"T"** for true or **"F"** for false alongside each of the following statements about asset management and asset-liability matching.

____ The asset management structure facilitates closer accounting between products and investments than is possible with more traditional investment operations.

____ The most important purpose of asset-liability matching from a regulator's viewpoint is to help make sure that each company meets its tax liability.

____ Asset-liability matching is particularly useful for newly introduced and untested products.

____ The cost of asset-liability management is particularly low when assets are managed along major product lines.

6. ____ True or False? Spin-off investment companies offer their services only to their parent companies.

Setting Investment Policy

7. List the individuals in the following groups who typically make up a company's investment committee.

Company executives ____

Outside directors ____

Circle the word in parentheses that correctly completes the following sentence:

The investment committee normally includes (more/fewer) company executives than outside directors.

8. List six factors that a company's investment committee typically considers when setting guidelines for investing the company's assets.

(1) ____

(2) ____

(3) ____

(4) ____

(5) ____

(6) ____

9. Name three people in an investment department who are responsible for developing the investment area's operational plans.

____

What qualifications do these investment professionals usually have?

____

10. In choosing investments, an insurance company portfolio manager generally considers a number of different factors. Identify and describe four of these factors.

____

____

____

____

Types of Investments

11. Common stock can be contrasted with preferred stock in a number of ways. Alongside each of the following statements, place either a **"C"** for common stock or a **"P"** for preferred stock to indicate which type of stock the statement best describes.

____ Holders of this type of stock may vote in the election of the company's board of directors.

____ Dividends are paid first to holders of this type of stock.

____ This type of stock offers greater capital gain potential.

____ Holders of this type of stock have a prior claim on the issuing company's assets if the company goes out of business and must sell its assets to pay its debts.

12. ____ True or False? In recent years, there has been a trend among regulators to place increasingly strict limitations upon the total percentage of common stocks that an insurer may include in its assets.

13. ____ True or False? Preferred stocks offer greater certainty of income to investors than do bonds.

14. Distinguish between the **stock market** in general and a **stock exchange** in particular.

____

____

15. Rhonda Ballew is a portfolio manager for the Harbinger Life Insurance Company. Ms. Ballew's approval authority for stock purchases is $500,000. If Ms. Ballew wants to undertake a stock purchase of more than $500,000, she must seek authorization from someone with more financial authority. Depending on how large Mr. Ballew's proposed stock purchase is, her request may be referred upward to Harbinger's

(1) ____________________ (2)____________________

(3) ____________________ (4)____________________

Identify one drawback of requiring authorization from the board of directors for a stock purchase.

____

16. Ed Blackwing is an investment analyst. If Mr. Blackwing is typical of many investment analysts, where does Mr. Blackwing obtain the information he needs to evaluate various investments?

____

17. ____ True or False? After deciding which stocks to buy, a portfolio manager then carries out his or her own buy and sell orders on the stock exchange floor.

18. For each pair of investments listed below, circle the investment that typically would offer a greater degree of safety of principal for its investors.

a. **junk bonds / preferred stocks**

b. **secured bonds / debentures**

c. **federal government bonds / other types of bonds**

From among the three investors listed below, circle the one who stands to gain the most from an increase in a company's profitability.

a bondholder / a common stockholder / a preferred stockholder

19. Hoyt Brookes, an experienced investor, has purchased bonds that he can either hold until their maturity or sell before they mature.

What factors control whether Mr. Brooks should hold onto or sell these bonds?

____

____

20. Cite two advantages to the issuer and one advantage to the investor of private placements of bonds.

advantages to the issuer

____

____

advantage to the investor

____

21. Identify several factors that determine what rating an agency gives to a bond.

____

____

22. ____ True or False? In general, the higher the bond rating, the lower the rate of return; the lower the bond rating, the higher the rate of return.

23. ____ True or False? In the United States, the interest rate on a mortgage loan can be fixed for up to 30 years, but in Canada, the interest rate is usually fixed for a shorter period, such as 6 months to 5 years.

24. In the United States, mortgages held by insurance companies are distributed among the types of property shown below. Rank the types of property that insurers own mortgages on, from the most commonly held type of property to the least commonly held type of property. Write **1, 2, 3,** or **4** alongside each type of property, using "1" for the property representing the greatest percentage of insurer mortgage loans and "4" for the property representing the smallest percentage of insurer mortgage loans.

____One- to four-family property ____Farm property

____Multifamily property ____Nonresidential property

25. What organizational structure is generally used by insurance companies for the direct acquisition of mortgages?

____

Once a mortgage loan is made, what steps are involved in administering or servicing the loan?

(1)________________________ (2)________________________

(3)________________________ (4)________________________

26. The Sunflower Life Insurance Company, a small company, acquires its mortgage investments through mortgage correspondents rather than through direct acquisition. What are two probable advantages to Sunflower of using mortgage correspondents?

____

____

27. Other than investing in individual mortgages, in what ways can an insurer invest in the mortgage market?

____

____

____

28. Write **"T"** for true or **"F"** for false alongside each of the following statements about real estate investments.

____ There is a current trend among regulatory authorities to tighten restrictions on real estate investment by insurers.

____ Real estate offers investors current income at rates that are higher than those paid on other equity investments.

____ Pension funds are investors that are well-suited to real estate investments because of their large cash flows and their long-term nature.

____ Real estate values fluctuate more than the values of common stocks or fixed-income bonds.

____ All of an insurer's real estate must be purchased either for the insurer's own use or as income-producing property.

____ Depreciating improved real estate has tax benefits for an insurer.

29. The Highrise Development Corporation built an office tower which it then sold to the Excelsior Life Insurance Company under a sale-and-leaseback agreement. How is this arrangement beneficial to

Highrise?____

Excelsior? ____

____

RELATIONSHIPS WITH OTHER DEPARTMENTS

30. Why must an insurer's executive staff and board of directors have a close relationship with the investment staff?

____

31. The product design task force of the Hominy Life Insurance Company sends an outline and description of a new product to Hominy's investment staff. What information is included in the description?

____

____

____

____

What information will the investment staff include in its report back to the product design task force?

____

To assess your understanding of the material in this chapter, go to the Test Preparation Guide (TPG) for this course and work the sample questions from this chapter. The TPG will explain how to study for and take examinations and will provide you with practice in answering the types of questions that appear on FLMI examinations. Be sure to check your answers to see how well you have mastered the material covered in this chapter. If you have not mastered the material, then reread the chapter in the assigned textbook and rework the corresponding exercises in this student guide. Then return to the TPG and rework the sample questions provided.

Chapter 13

The Accounting Function

To help you prepare for the FLMI examination for this course, read the entire preface of this student guide. It contains many practical pointers that will help you in studying FLMI educational material. This student guide is designed to help you learn the material covered in the assigned textbook. Working the exercises in this student guide is not a substitute for reading the book. Be sure to read the assigned chapter in the book before completing the exercises in the corresponding chapter of the student guide. Consult the current LOMA Insurance Education Catalog for the correct text assignment for this course.

CHAPTER OVERVIEW

The accounting function provides an insurance company's management with information about the company's financial soundness and performance. Many external parties also are interested in reports issued by the accounting area.

In Chapter 13, you read about the fundamentals of accounting and some accounting reports. In addition, you learned about insurance company accounting functions and practices, and ways that accounting is helpful in company analysis, planning, and control. You read about ways that insurance accounting differs from commercial accounting. Finally, you were introduced to budgeting and auditing.

After studying this chapter, you should be able to

- Identify the parties that use or are interested in accounting information
- Define the term solvency and explain why this concept is particularly important to insurance companies
- Describe the responsibilities of the company's controller and the rest of the accounting staff
- Identify the elements of the basic accounting equation and explain their relationship and interaction during an accounting transaction
- Distinguish between statutory accounting practices (SAP) and generally accepted accounting principles (GAAP)
- Identify three accounting reports that most companies issue

- State the purpose of separate, or segregated, accounts
- Explain the purposes of financial analysis and auditing

Outline of Major Topics Covered in this Chapter

I. Who Uses Accounting Information?
II. Accounting Personnel and Their Activities
    A. Titles of Accounting Staff Members
    B. Types of Accounting
    C. Accounting Staff Responsibilities
III. Accounting Fundamentals
    A. The Basic Accounting Equation
    B. Accounting Terminology
    C. Accounting Principles
IV. Accounting Reports and Statements
    A. Accounting Reports
        1. Balance sheet
        2. Income statement
        3. Annual report
    B. The Annual Statement
        1. The Annual Statement in the United States
        2. The Annual Statement in Canada
V. Unique Aspects of Life and Health Insurance Accounting
    A. Accrual-basis and Cash-basis Accounting
    B. Suspense Accounts
    C. Nonledger Accounts
    D. Nonadmitted Assets
VI. Types of Accounting in Insurance Companies
    A. Policy Accounting
        1. Premium billing and collection
            a. Ordinary premiums
            b. Group premiums
            c. Industrial insurance premiums
        2. Commissions
        3. Policy loans
        4. Policy dividends
        5. Claim accounting
    B. Investment Accounting
        1. Separate accounts and general accounts
            a. Segmentation of general accounts
    C. General Accounting
        1. Payroll accounting
        2. Disbursements
    D. Tax Accounting
VII. Planning and Controlling Financial Operations
    A. Financial Analysis
    B. Budget Planning
        1. Types of budgets
            a. The revenue budget
            b. Expense budgets
    C. Budgets as Evaluation and Control Devices

D. Auditing
   1. Internal auditing unit
   2. External auditors
   3. Auditing methods

Review of Key Terms and Concepts

Define the following key terms and concepts:

accounting (p. 357)____

____

solvency (p. 358)____

____

assets (p. 361)____

____

liabilities (p. 361)_______________________________________

____

owner's equity (p. 361)____________________________________

____

account (p. 362)____

____

debit (p. 363)____

____

credit (p. 363)____

____

journal (p. 363)____

____

ledger (p. 363)____

____

going-concern concept (p. 364)______________________________

____

balance sheet (p. 365) ____________________

____

income statement (p. 366) ____________________

____

annual report (p. 367) ____________________

____

Annual Statement (p. 367) ____________________

____

accrual-basis accounting (p. 371) ____________________

____

cash-basis accounting (p. 371) ____________________

____

suspense account (p. 372) ____________________

____

nonledger account (p. 372) ____________________

____

nonadmitted asset (p. 372) ____________________

____

policy accounting (p. 373) ____________________

____

preauthorized payment (p. 374) ____________________

____

lock-box banking (p. 375) ____________________

____

self-administered billing plan (p. 375) ____________________

____

insurer-administered billing plan (p. 375) ____________________

____

cash premium accounting (p. 376) ____________________

____

advance and arrears accounting (p. 376) ____________________

____

separate (segregated) account (p. 378) ____________________

____

segmentation (p. 379) ____________________

____

financial analysis (p. 382) ____________________

____

ratio analysis (p. 383) ____________________

____

budget (p. 383) ____________________

____

revenue budget (p. 384) ____________________

____

benefits budget (p. 384) ____________________

____

sales expense budget (p. 384) ____________________

____

general and administrative expense budget (p. 384) ____________________

____

auditing (p. 386) ____________________

____

internal audit (p. 386)____

____

external audit (p. 386)____

____

WORKING OUTLINE

Who Uses Accounting Information?

1. Why are the following people or groups outside a company's accounting area interested in accounting information?

   Board members, officers, and managers______________________________

   ____

   Other company employees____

   ____

   Company owners____

   ____

   Insurance consumers____

   ____

   Creditors and potential creditors____________________________________

   ____

   Government agencies____

   ____

2. Why is solvency particularly important to insurance companies?

   ____

   ____

ACCOUNTING PERSONNEL AND THEIR ACTIVITIES

3. Susan Rogo, Emerald Life Insurance Company's controller, is responsible for most of Emerald's major accounting functions. Identify four areas for which Ms. Rogo is responsible.

(1) ____________________ (2) ____________________

(3) ____________________ (4) ____________________

Emerald's internal auditing unit reports directly to the auditing committee rather than to Ms. Rogo. Why?

____

ACCOUNTING FUNDAMENTALS

4. State the basic accounting equation.

____________ = ____________ + ____________

* * *

5. For each transaction below, restate the basic accounting equation using the appropriate dollar amounts in each blank. The first blanks are filled in for you. (Answers to 5b, 5c, and 5d are at the end of the chapter.)

(a) Tom Pickard and Jill Carter form a business by investing $3,000 of their own money.

$3,000 = 0 + $3,000

(b) The business purchases merchandise on credit for $500.

____________ = ____________ + ____________

(c) The business sells all the merchandise for $800.

____________ = ____________ + ____________

(d) The business pays its creditor the $500 it owes.

____________ = ____________ + ____________

____ True or False? The transactions above violate the principle of double-entry bookkeeping.

* * *

6. ____ True or False? In a traditional T-account, credits increase asset and expense accounts, but decrease liability, income, and owners' equity accounts.

The following questions apply to the different accounting practices and principles that insurers use and follow.

7a. Distinguish between statutory accounting practices (SAP) and generally accepted accounting practices (GAAP).

____

____

____

7b. What assumptions are made as to the future of the company

in SAP?______________________________________

in GAAP?_____________________________________

7c. Do insurance companies in the United States use SAP, GAAP, or both SAP and GAAP? Why?

____

____

7d. What accounting practices do Canadian insurers use?

____

____

* * *

Accounting Reports and Statements

8. Identify five accounting reports that are prepared solely for an insurance company's management.

(1) ____________________ (2) ____________________

(3) ____________________ (4) ____________________

(5) ____________________

9. ____ True or False? To be in balance, a balance sheet must show that the total of assets and owner's equity equals the total amount of liabilities.

10. ____ True or False? A company's profit or loss depends on the relationship between income and expenses.

11. Circle the words/phrases that correctly complete the following statements:

Any company that is (publicly owned/privately owned) is required to prepare an annual report for its owners. This annual report is typically prepared according to (SAP/GAAP).

12. Who determines the format and content of the Annual Statement

in Canada?______________________________

in the United States?______________________________

13. Place an **"X"** in the space beside each item that is a component of the Annual Statement in the United States.

____ a summary of operations (statement of income and expenses)

____ a surplus statement

____ a balance sheet in the form of an assets page and a liabilities, capital, and surplus page

____ supporting exhibits, schedules, and supplemental reports

14. ____ True or False? An insurer that does business in the United States must file its Annual Statement in each state in which it is licensed to do business.

15. ____ True or False? In addition to filing an Annual Statement with the federal Department of Insurance, an insurer that operates in Canada must file an Annual Statement in only the first province in which it became licensed to do business.

UNIQUE ASPECTS OF LIFE AND HEALTH INSURANCE ACCOUNTING

16. ____ True or False? In contrast to accrual-basis accounting, entries are made in cash-basis accounting only when cash actually changes hands.

17. ____ True or False? Cash-basis accounting is used in some insurance companies because of the bilateral nature of the insurance contract.

18. The Generation Life Insurance Company uses the cash-basis accounting method. However, not every cash transaction that occurs can be processed fully. Briefly describe a situation in which Generation may receive a cash payment that it does not immediately consider as income.

____

____

____

19. The most important nonledger account that appears on the Annual Statement is the policy reserve -- an insurance company's largest liability. Place an "X" alongside each of the following nonledger assets or liabilities that must also appear on the Annual Statement:

____ deferred and uncollected premiums

____ furniture and office equipment

____ dividends due and accrued

____ federal income taxes

____ personal income taxes of all outside directors

____ investment income due and accrued

Types of Accounting in Insurance Companies

20. Next to each of the following descriptions regarding policy accounting, indicate with a "T" or an "F" whether each statement is true or false.

____ Policy accounting is responsible for the largest number of transactions within an insurance company.

____ All insurers' accounting systems provide for automatic updates of agents' commission records when premiums are collected.

____ Policy loan accounting involves ensuring that the total amount of a policy loan's principal plus interest does not exceed the policy's cash value.

21. In the blank space to the right of the items listed below, state the steps that the policy accounting staff would take when dividends become payable for the policyowners identified in the left-hand column.

(a) Jeff Jacobs elected to receive payment of his policy dividends in cash.

(b) Tammy Haigler requested that her dividends be applied to pay policy premiums as they come due.

(c) Charlotte Bean chose to leave her dividends with the company to accumulate at interest.

(d) Bob Carloch elected to have his dividends used to purchase paid-up additions.

(e) Leslie Cook requested that his dividends be used to purchase one-year term insurance.

22. ____ True or False? A claim reserve account must be established and maintained for claims about which an insurer has been notified but for which no payment has yet been made.

23. ____ True or False? Investments provide the largest source of insurer income.

24. What is the purpose of a separate or segregated account, and what benefits do they offer an insurer over traditional pooled accounts?

____

____

____

25. Anna Friedrich is manager of the payroll accounting area at the Amethyst Life Insurance Company. Ms. Friedrich's staff is responsible for

(1) ____________________ (2) ____________________

(3) ____________________ (4) ____________________

Amethyst's payroll records contain information about each employee's

____

26. In the space provided below, write in some types of disbursements that apply to each of the following categories:

Policy	Compensation	Investment	General operations

Tax Accounting

27. Next to each of the following descriptions regarding policy accounting, indicate with a "T" or an "F" whether each statement is true or false.

____ State and provincial governments impose premium taxes on insurers as a percentage of the claims that each insurer pays out.

____ In the United States, all states impose premium taxes on the same basis.

____ All Canadian provinces levy a tax on life insurance premiums.

Planning and Controlling Financial Operations

28. Briefly explain why financial analyses are useful to

a company's officers and managers______________________________

____

industry analysts____

____

brokerage houses____

____

state and provincial regulators________________________________

____

the NAIC____

____

29. Match the item in the left-hand column to the item in the

right-hand column that completes a type of comparison or a ratio that insurers use to measure financial performance in a process called ratio analysis. Draw a line from each item in Column A to the appropriate item in Column B. (For example [shown below], one ratio that insurers use is **actual investment yield** to **anticipated investment yield.**)

Column A		Column B
actual investment yield	————	anticipated investment yield
benefit disbursements		investment income
sales production		budgeted expenses
cash surrender value		premium income
actual expenses		anticipated claim costs
claim costs		premium income
investment expenses		sales targets

30. In order to achieve a well-planned budget and budgeting process, company personnel should cooperate in these areas:

____

____

____

31. ____ True or False? A cash receipts and disbursements budget helps to allocate funds for significant purchases.

____ True or False? A capital expenditures budget helps to monitor cash flow.

32. Why must the revenue budget be completed before other budgets?

____

33. Conrad Dayal is an auditor with the Searchlight Life Insurance Company. What are some of Mr. Dayal's responsibilities with respect to ensuring the reliability of Searchlight's financial reports?

____

____

____

34. ____ True or False? Internal auditors examine only those company affairs that have to do with the expenditure of funds.

35. After an internal auditor has completed the examination of an area, the auditor will submit a detailed report. What types of information will be contained in the auditor's report?

____

____

36. Briefly describe the audit requirements prescribed by regulatory authorities for companies in

the United States______________________________

Canada______________________________

37. ____ True or False? Auditors consider statistical sampling an inefficient tool for examining a company's financial condition.

ANSWERS TO SELECTED QUESTIONS

5b. \$3,500 (assets) = \$500 (liabilities) + \$3,000 (owner's equity)

5c. \$3,800 (assets) = \$500 (liabilities) + \$3,300 (owner's equity)

5d. \$3,300 (assets) = 0 (liabilities) + \$3,300 (owner's equity)

To assess your understanding of the material in this chapter, go to the Test Preparation Guide (TPG) for this course and work the sample questions from this chapter. The TPG will explain how to study for and take examinations and will provide you with practice in answering the types of questions that appear on FLMI examinations. Be sure to check your answers to see how well you have mastered the material covered in this chapter. If you have not mastered the material, then reread the chapter in the assigned textbook and rework the corresponding exercises in this student guide. Then return to the TPG and rework the sample questions provided.

Chapter 14

Legal Operations

To help you prepare for the FLMI examination for this course, read the entire preface of this student guide. It contains many practical pointers that will help you in studying FLMI educational material. This student guide is designed to help you learn the material covered in the assigned textbook. Working the exercises in this student guide is not a substitute for reading the book. Be sure to read the assigned chapter in the book before completing the exercises in the corresponding chapter of the student guide. Consult the current LOMA Insurance Education Catalog for the correct text assignment for this course.

CHAPTER OVERVIEW

An insurance company's legal staff assists in the company's operations by ensuring both that the company fulfills all of its legal responsibilities and that the company's own rights are protected.

Chapter 14 described the manner in which insurance company legal staffs are organized, what functions they perform, and the relationships of the legal department with other areas of the company. You learned about how lawyers are involved in governmental relations and you found out about cases in which a company may need outside counsel. You also read about equal opportunity legislation in the United States and Canada.

After studying this chapter, you should be able to

- Describe the different ways to organize a legal department in a life and health insurance company
- Discuss the different responsibilities assigned to life and health insurance company lawyers and legal staff
- Differentiate among and describe the areas of law with which an insurance company's legal department is concerned
- Describe several ways in which the legal department interacts with other insurance company functional areas

Outline of Major Topics Covered in this Chapter

I. Organizational Structures of Legal Departments

A. Factors Affecting Size of the Legal Department
B. Traditional Structure
C. Regional Structure
    1. Maintaining governmental relations
    2. Assisting the claim department
    3. Arranging for outside counsel
D. Functional Structure

II. Legal Department Functions
A. Insurance Law
B. Contract Law
    1. Policy drafting
    2. Claims
C. Agency Law
D. Securities Law
E. Employment Law
    1. Classifications of employment law
    2. Equal employment opportunity in the United States
    3. Equal employment opportunity in Canada
F. Tax Law
    1. Personal income tax law
    2. Employee benefits tax law
    3. Estate tax law
    4. Corporate income tax law
G. Real Property Law
H. Corporate Law
I. Administrative Law
J. Litigation

III. Additional Responsibilities

Review of Key Terms and Concepts

Define the following key terms and concepts:

paralegal (p. 391)____

____

bar examination (p. 391)____

____

outside counsel (p. 393)____

____

contract (p. 397)____

____

contract law (p. 397)____

____

bilateral contract (p. 398)

unilateral contract (p. 398)

agency law (p. 400)

securities law (p. 400)

human rights law (p. 402)

employment standards law (p. 402)

pension benefits law (p. 402)

collective bargaining (p. 402)

Equal Employment Opportunity Commission (EEOC) (p. 402)

disparate treatment (p. 403)

disparate impact (p. 403)

perpetuation of past discrimination (p. 403)

back pay (p. 403)

personal income tax law (p. 404)________________________________

____

estate tax law (p. 405)____

____

corporate income tax law (p. 406)_______________________________

____

real property law (p. 406)______________________________________

____

administrative law (p. 408)_____________________________________

____

litigation (p. 408)____

____

punitive damages (p. 409)_______________________________________

____

compensatory damages (p. 409)___________________________________

____

WORKING OUTLINE

Organizational Structures of Legal Departments

1. Margaret O'Malley is vice president and general counsel for the Shamrock Life Insurance Company, a large insurance company whose legal department is organized in the traditional organizational structure. Place an **"O"** in the blank alongside each responsibility in the right-hand column below that probably falls to Ms. O'Malley herself.

    ____ Delegating work to appropriate legal staff members

    ____ Conducting legal research on routine claim investigations

    ____ Serving as advisor to Shamrock's board of directors

    ____ Overseeing the work of the legal department staff

2. ____ True or False? Large insurers in the United States have gradually moved more and more legal functions to regional offices, so that nearly every traditional home office legal function can now be found in some regional office.

3. The Spartacus Life Insurance Company maintains a legal staff in each of its regional offices. List some ways in which decentralization of the legal function can help Spartacus to

maintain governmental relations ______________________________

____

assist the claim department ______________________________

____

arrange for outside counsel ______________________________

____

4. In response to the increasing complexity of the insurance business, many insurers have begun assigning lawyers to specific functional or product areas throughout the company. Give two examples of product areas that might have a substantial need for legal advice.

   (1) ____

   (2) ____

5. ____ True or False? A functional structure in a company's legal operations concentrates the efforts of home office attorneys, thereby making the central legal department organization larger and more unwieldy.

LEGAL DEPARTMENT FUNCTIONS

6. Insurance law affects all other types of law with respect to insurance matters. In the spaces provided below, indicate with a **"Y"** (yes) or an **"N"** (no) whether insurance laws affect each area for potential legal disputes.

   ____ Licensing of insurers and agents in every jurisdiction in which they do business

   ____ The insurer's dealings with agents, employees, policyowners, and proposed insureds

   ____ The drafting of insurance contracts

   ____ The payment of claims

7. In the following section, contrast unilateral contracts with bilateral contracts. For each question listed in the left-hand column, write in the space provided in the right-hand columns the answers as they apply to each type of contract. Write answers to each question in one or both columns.

	Unilateral contract	Bilateral contract
Who has made promises?		
What are the possible consequences if a party to the contract fails to live up to the promises made?		
What happens if a policyowner fails to pay premiums due?		

* * *

Policies are initially drafted by an insurer's marketing specialists and actuaries. Then the drafts are reviewed by company lawyers and, in the United States, by the appropriate regulatory agencies.

8a. Why do company lawyers review policy drafts?

____

____

8b. What options does an insurer have if the state insurance department does not approve a policy draft?

(1) ____

(2) ____

(3) ____

9. ____ True or False? In Canada, insurers must submit all policies for formal approval in every province in which the product will be sold.

10. ____ True or False? Simplified policy language has been mandated throughout the United States and Canada.

* * *

11. Fred Mishler is an insurance company lawyer who specializes in agency law. Identify Mr. Mishler's duties as to

agency agreements____

improper actions by an agent________________________________

12. In the following groups of sentences, circle the words and phrases that correctly complete the sentences.

As more investment-oriented products are developed, insurers come under (decreased/increased) scrutiny from the SEC. Laws (allow/prohibit) the sale of certain variable annuities by agents (with/without) SEC licenses.

Canadian companies who sell investment products in the United States (are/are not) required to comply with SEC regulations. Variable products sold in Canada must be approved by (the SEC/provincial Departments of Insurance). In order to sell mutual funds in Canada, agents must be accredited by the applicable provincial (securities commissions/Departments of Insurance).

13. For each of the following statements, indicate in the space provided whether each statement is true or false by writing a **"T"** or an **"F"**.

____ Insurance company lawyers help to negotiate the terms of agreements for private placements and the purchase of stocks and bonds.

____ When an insurer issues its own company stock, the company lawyers monitor company action to ensure compliance with applicable regulations.

____ Most of a legal department's work in the area of employment law is conducted for outside individuals and companies.

14. Human rights laws specifically prohibit unfair job discrimination on the basis of several factors. Identify six such factors.

(1) ________________________ (2)________________________

(3) ________________________ (4)________________________

(5) ________________________ (6)________________________

15. Place an **"X"** alongside each action that the Equal Employment Opportunity Commission (EEOC) is empowered to take in answer to a job discrimination complaint.

____ Investigate the complaint

____ Negotiate with all interested parties to try to reach an agreement about the alleged discrimination

____ Hold a public hearing on the complaint

____ File a suit in a court of law on behalf of the aggrieved individual

____ Order an employer to discontinue a discriminatory action

16. Decide whether each person in the following situations is a victim of one of these forms of discrimination: **disparate impact, disparate treatment**, or **perpetuation of past discrimination.** In the blank space to the right of each situation, write your decision. If you decide that no discrimination has occurred, write **"none"** in the blank space.

    Mary Carroll was denied a job as a secretary because of her poor typing and telephone skills.

    Martin Roma, who was otherwise well qualified for a job as a customer service representative, was not hired because he was 59 years old.

    Although Virginia Roberts was the most qualified candidate for Agency Manager, she was not promoted to the position that came open in 1992 because the company, in its 50-year history, had always maintained a practice of promoting only males to the rank of agency manager.

    Ernest Stedding, whose typing skills were excellent, was denied a job as a typist in a typing unit because all the other typists were women.

17. Once a company has been found guilty of discrimination by a court, what remedies might the court order?

    (1) ________________________________

    (2) ________________________________

18. Identify and briefly describe two acts that specifically prohibit age discrimination and discrimination against disabled people.

    (1) ________________________________

    ____

    (2) ________________________________

    ____

19. Circle the words that correctly complete the sentence below.

The federal and provincial governments in Canada have passed human rights acts that prohibit employment discrimination on the basis of an individual's

race	color	religion or creed	age
health	national origin	marital status	sex

20. Circle the word in parentheses that correctly completes the following sentence:

The enforcement of human rights legislation in Canada is the responsibility of (federal/provincial) human rights commissions.

21. Briefly discuss the steps that Canadian human rights commissions may take when an individual is determined to have a valid discrimination complaint.

____

____

22. Laura Shimberg is an attorney for Long Life Insurance Company who specializes in personal income tax law. How can Ms. Shimberg's knowledge of personal income tax law help her in arranging compensation packages to attract top executives to join Long Life?

____

____

23. ____ True or False? Some employee benefits that are deductible from an employer's taxable income are not taxable to employees who receive the benefits.

24. Circle the word(s) that correctly complete the following sentence:

Funds paid in a lump sum to the beneficiary of a life insurance policy (are/are not) subject to estate tax.

25. Corporate income tax lawyers help company accountants interpret tax laws that apply to insurance companies. This helps the accountants to

calculate the company's________________________________

and to maximize the company's____________________________.

26. Harry Chitwood is a real estate attorney in an insurance company's legal department. Write an "X" in the blank beside each task that Mr. Chitwood might be called upon to perform.

____ Handle contracts and deeds for the purchase and sale of property

____ Negotiate contracts for buying and selling mortgages

____ Advise the underwriting department about risk selection

____ Handle foreclosure proceedings

____ Advise the investment department about real estate assets

____ Negotiate to acquire land for development

____ Draft and review sales and rental agreements for a company development

27. How might a corporate lawyer be useful to a company during a merger or takeover?

(1) ____

(2) ____

(3) ____

28. Briefly describe a corporate law specialist's activities with regard to mutualizing or demutualizing a company.

____

____

* * *

Indicate in the space next to each of the following statements whether each statement is true or false.

29. ____ Regulatory commissions or agencies invite company lawyers to appear before them, to comment on proposed insurance regulations, or to otherwise render advice.

30. ____ Company lawyers with administrative law duties spend most of their time seeking regulators' approval of such items as policy forms, rates, and advertising materials.

31. ____ All insurance companies rely solely on outside counsel to handle litigation.

* * *

32a. John Gartin, a lawyer who specializes in litigation, is in charge of defending the Mammoth Life Insurance Company against a suit brought by a disgruntled tenant who leases space in one of Mammoth's office towers. List some responsibilities that Mr. Gartin has as litigator of this lawsuit.

____

____

____

32b. Mr. Gartin probably will try to settle the case before the trial actually begins. State two reasons that a trial may be detrimental to Mammoth, even if Mammoth wins the case.

(1) ____

(2) ____

32c. If the case goes to trial and Mammoth loses, and if the court decides that Mammoth acted in bad faith in dealing with the tenant who brought the suit, what sorts of penalties could the court inflict on Mammoth?

(1) ____________________ (2) ____________________

* * *

ADDITIONAL RESPONSIBILITIES

33. How does the legal department work with the marketing department in the areas of

agent contracts ______________________________

commission schedules ______________________________

agent training ______________________________

sales calls ______________________________

advertising materials ______________________________

34. ____ True or False? The legal staff helps the underwriting department by monitoring laws regarding discrimination and privacy.

35. List three non-insurance functions that insurance company lawyers are often called upon to perform.

(1) ____

(2) ____

(3) ____

To assess your understanding of the material in this chapter, go to the Test Preparation Guide (TPG) for this course and work the sample questions from this chapter. The TPG will explain how to study for and take examinations and will provide you with practice in answering the types of questions that appear on FLMI examinations. Be sure to check your answers to see how well you have mastered the material covered in this chapter. If you have not mastered the material, then reread the chapter in the assigned textbook and rework the corresponding exercises in this student guide. Then return to the TPG and rework the sample questions provided.

Chapter 15

The Human Resources Function

To help you prepare for the FLMI examination for this course, read the entire preface of this student guide. It contains many practical pointers that will help you in studying FLMI educational material. This student guide is designed to help you learn the material covered in the assigned textbook. Working the exercises in this student guide is not a substitute for reading the book. Be sure to read the assigned chapter in the book before completing the exercises in the corresponding chapter of the student guide. Consult the current LOMA Insurance Education Catalog for the correct text assignment for this course.

CHAPTER OVERVIEW

An organization cannot function without its people -- that is, its human resources. Chapter 15 discussed all aspects of the human resources function within a company, beginning with human resources planning, forecasting, needs assessment, and recruitment. You read about employee orientation, training, and development, how staff performance is evaluated, and the different ways employees may be separated from the company. Finally, you learned how companies establish and administer compensation systems.

After studying this chapter, you should be able to

- Describe the functions of the human resources area
- Explain the steps involved in human resource planning
- Compare the benefits and drawbacks of internal and external recruiting
- Describe the steps involved in the employee selection process and different types of selection tests
- Compare training, orientation, and professional development
- Describe some performance appraisal techniques and the benefits and drawbacks of each one
- Identify the factors considered in determining employee compensation

Outline of Major Topics Covered in this Chapter

I. Duties of the Human Resources Function
II. Human Resource Planning
    A. Forecasting Staffing Needs
        1. Forecasting techniques
            a. Trend analysis
            b. Ratio analysis
    B. Estimating the Labor Supply
        1. Internal labor supply
        2. External labor supply
III. Recruiting Qualified Personnel
    A. Internal Recruitment
    B. External Recruitment
        1. Sources of external candidates
            a. Help-wanted advertising
            b. Private employment agencies
            c. Educational institutions
            d. Staff referrals
    C. Selecting Employees
        1. The application form
        2. The screening interview
        3. Employment testing
        4. The employment interview
        5. Reference checks and physical examinations
            a. Reference checks
            b. Physical examinations
IV. Orientation, Training, and Development
    A. Orientation
    B. Training and Development
        1. Training and Development Methods
            a. On-the-job training
            b. On-the-job development techniques
            c. Training and development conducted "off-the-job"
V. Evaluating Staff Performance
    A. Performance Appraisal Methods
        1. Essay appraisal
        2. Critical incident technique
        3. Ranking methods
        4. Graphic rating scales
        5. Behaviorally anchored rating scales (BARS)
VI. Separation of Employees
VII. Establishing Compensation Systems
    A. Job Evaluation
    B. Wage and Salary Administration
        1. Pay incentives
    C. Benefits and Services

Review of Key Terms and Concepts

Define the following key terms and concepts:

human resource planning (p. 416) ____________________

____

trend analysis (p. 417) ____________________

____

ratio analysis (p. 418) ____________________

____

skills inventory (p. 419) ____________________

____

succession chart (p. 419) ____________________

____

promotion (p. 423) ____________________

____

upgrading (p. 423) ____________________

____

lateral transfer (p. 423) ____________________

____

demotion (p. 423) ____________________

____

job posting (p. 424) ____________________

____

position description (p. 424) ____________________

____

help-wanted advertising (p. 425) ____________________

____

private employment agency (p. 425) ____________________

____

temporary help agency (p. 425) ____

____

executive search firm (p. 425) ____

____

staff referral (p. 427) ____

____

application form (p. 427) ____

____

screening interview (p. 430) ____

____

validity (p. 430) ____

____

reliability (p. 430) ____

____

aptitude test (p. 431) ____

____

biodata (p. 431) ____

____

performance test (p. 431) ____

____

work sample test (p. 431) ____

____

situation management test (p. 431) ____

____

personality test (p. 431) ____

____

interest test (p. 431)____________________

____

employment interview (p. 432)____________________

____

orientation (p. 433)____________________

____

training (p. 433)____________________

____

development (p. 433)____________________

____

learning objectives (p. 437)____________________

____

job aid (p. 437)____________________

____

on-the-job training (p. 437)____________________

____

job rotation (p. 438)____________________

____

plateau (p. 439)____________________

____

lecture (p. 439)____________________

____

conference method (p. 440)____________________

____

case study (p. 440)____________________

____

role playing (p. 440) ______________________________

____

programmed instruction (p. 440) ______________________________

____

computer-based training (p. 440) ______________________________

____

essay appraisal technique (p. 442) ______________________________

____

critical incident technique (p. 442) ______________________________

____

alternation ranking method (p. 442) ______________________________

____

paired comparison method (p. 443) ______________________________

____

graphic rating scale (p. 443) ______________________________

____

behaviorally anchored rating scale (BARS) (p. 443) ______________________________

____

separation (p. 445) ______________________________

____

resignation (p. 445) ______________________________

____

layoff (p. 445) ______________________________

____

retirement (p. 445) ______________________________

____

discharge (p. 445) ____

____

exit interview (p. 446) ____

____

outplacement counseling (p. 446) _________________________________

____

point factor comparison system (p. 447) ___________________________

____

production bonus (p. 448) ____

____

profit-sharing plan (p. 448) ______________________________________

____

current profit-sharing plan (p. 448) ______________________________

____

deferred profit-sharing plan (p. 448) _____________________________

____

employee stock ownership plan (ESOP) (p. 448) ____________________

____

WORKING OUTLINE

1. Name five duties common to most life and health insurance company human resource functions.

 ____

 ____

 ____

 ____

 ____

Human Resource Planning

2. Human resource planning is becoming increasingly challenging because of these two changing factors:

   (1) ______________________________ (2) ______________________________

3. Place an **"X"** beside each of the following factors that a company considers when forecasting staffing needs:

   ____ The demand for a company's products

   ____ The performance of current employees

   ____ New products

   ____ Technological developments

   ____ Trends in labor force demographics

   ____ Economic factors

   ____ The company's expected financial condition

   ____ The company's long-range plans

4. ____ True or False? The quantitative forecasting techniques of trend analysis and ratio analysis are used more often in small companies than in large companies.

5. Draw a line from the forecasting technique named in the left-hand column to the appropriate description of that technique in the right-hand column.

Trend analysis	Agency manager Joe Swinson knows that for the past five years seven new agents were added to the sales force each year. Mr. Swinson therefore assumes that seven new agents will be added in the current year as well.
Ratio analysis	Claim manager Sally Carver knows that a claim entry clerk can enter 75 claims a day. If Ms. Carver's staff receives an average of 300 claims a day, then she divides 300 by 75 to determine how many entry clerks are needed to do the work.

6. The typical skills inventory maintained by some human resources departments contains the following information about employees:

   ___job performance evaluations ___aptitude test results

___health information ___work experience

___general salary history ___education

___professional organization memberships ___training

7. Succession charts benefit managers by enabling them to

identify____

plan____

motivate____

8. Estimating the number of people outside a company who might have certain job qualifications can be done by monitoring such factors as local and national economic developments, expected unemployment rates, and numbers of recent high school or college graduates with certain skills. This information can be obtained from

(1) ____________________ (2)____________________

(3) ____________________ (4)____________________

RECRUITING QUALIFIED PERSONNEL

Companies recruit job candidates from both inside and outside a company.

9. Draw a line from the method of internal recruitment listed in the left-hand column to the appropriate description of that recruitment method in the right-hand column.

Promotion	Don Coleman's job title and duties were changed from vice president of accounting to assistant vice president after a takeover of his company by another company.
Upgrading	Susan Hoffman was elevated in the organizational hierarchy from senior claim examiner to claim manager.
Lateral transfer	Clarice Bhawana, an accountant, was retrained to fulfill the new, broader duties of her job when the accounting department was automated.
Demotion	Mario Ferrari, a junior claim examiner, was transferred to the underwriting department as a junior underwriter.

10. List five benefits of internal recruitment.

(1) ____

(2) ____

(3) ____

(4) ____

(5) ____

11. Identify one potential problem that can occur when internal recruitment is conducted informally.

____

12. ____ True or False? Internal job posting should never be done concurrently with external recruitment.

13. Some of the benefits of internal recruiting can become drawbacks that a company must counterbalance through external recruiting. List two negative features of internal recruiting that do not exist with external recruiting.

(1) ____

(2) ____

14. Circle the words and phrases that correctly complete the following sentence:

Help-wanted advertising is especially useful when unemployment is (high/low) and the demands of a job are (very demanding/not overly demanding).

15. ____ True or False? The fee that a private employment agency charges is usually paid by the employee, but the employee can receive a refund of part or all of the fee within a certain period if he or she is unhappy with the job.

16. Certain types of private employment agencies usually specialize in filling certain types of jobs. Decide which kind of agency -- a temporary help agency or an executive search firm -- would be more likely to fill each job below. Fill in the blanks with either **"TH"** for temporary help agency or **"ES"** for executive search firm.

____ upper-level managers

____ clerical workers

____ seasonal accounting jobs

____ underwriters

____ actuaries

____ executives

17. Identify one benefit and one potential problem of using staff referrals as a source of new employees.

benefit ____

potential problem ____________________________________

18. List some types of information that are requested on a typical job application form.

(1) ____________________ (2) ____________________

(3) ____________________ (4) ____________________

(5) ____________________ (6) ____________________

19. In the section below, circle the topics that should not be asked about on a job application form because of the possibility that asking for information on such topics can later lead to a charge of discrimination:

work experience	religious affiliation	past salaries	age
marital status	educational background	national origin	address

20. Compare an employment interview with a screening interview by answering the following questions for each type of interview.

	screening interview	**employment interview**
Who conducts the interview?		
What is the purpose of each?		

21. ____ True or False? Employment tests used for selection purposes must comply, as appropriate, with applicable regulations in the United States and Canada.

22. Circle the word that correctly completes the following sentence:

The clerical aptitude test is among the (most/least) commonly used aptitude tests in insurance companies.

23. ____ True or False? Performance tests are usually standardized and are used by many companies without modification.

24. On the next page, draw a line from each type of employment test listed in the left-hand column to the appropriate statement or description from the right-hand column that best fits each type of test.

situation management test

integrity test

work sample test

interest test

Job Effectiveness Prediction System (JEPS)

This test can be used as a career development tool after an applicant has been hired.

This test involves the presentation of a work-related situation either on paper, verbally, or on videotape, and the applicant is evaluated according to his or her response to the presentation.

This type of test could be in the form of an honesty test or a psychological assessment.

In this test, an applicant performs a task that is a necessary part of the job that the applicant seeks.

This test measures the aptitude of an entry-level clerical or technical-professional applicant who is seeking a nonsales position.

25. Why have personality tests been criticized?

26. What rights does an applicant have with regard to letters of reference

in Canada?

in the United States?

Why are some employers reluctant to provide business references for past employees?

27. What impact has the Americans with Disabilities Act (ADA) had on U.S. companies' physical examination requirements for job applicants?

ORIENTATION, TRAINING, AND DEVELOPMENT

The following questions relate to the employee orientation process in life and health insurance companies.

28a. The orientation process is usually a joint effort by the human resources staff and the new employee's department. Cite several kinds of information that the human resources staff may include in its orientation for new employees.

(1)____________________ (2)____________________

(3)____________________ (4)____________________

28b. What steps are involved in a new employee's typical orientation to his or her work area?

28c. Briefly describe the materials that may be used to introduce an employee to the insurance industry if he or she is new to the field.

28d. Who develops orientation materials for new employees?

* * *

29. In assessing training needs, a human resources specialist looks for areas in which there is a difference between the

knowledge and skills that employees currently have and the

employees' daily performance and their____________________

organization's current performance and its____________________

30. There are several possible approaches to assessing training and development needs. Briefly discuss the following five approaches.

analysis of specific job requirements____________________

analysis of work performance ______________________________

____

analysis of performance standards ______________________________

____

administration of an organization opinion survey ______________________________

____

organizational analysis ______________________________

____

31. Differentiate between training and development.

____

____

32. Cite three advantages of traditional on-the-job training (OJT).

(1) ______________________________

(2) ______________________________

(3) ______________________________

33. Circle the words in parentheses that correctly complete the following sentence:

Job rotation or cross-training (increases/decreases) the variety of tasks that an employee can perform, and (increases/decreases) the complexity of the employee's job at any one time.

34. Draw a line from the on-the-job development technique listed in the left-hand column to the appropriate description of that technique in the right-hand column.

coaching	A junior manager or potential manager candidate is assigned to work with an experienced manager. The junior employee is given some of the manager's work and responsibility and the manager instructs and encourages him or her.
understudy	A junior manager works with an experienced manager with the specific goal of training the junior employee to take over the job of the manager.

35. Circle the word(s) in bold that correctly complete the following passage.

Lee Shobin is a management trainee for the Exertion Life Insurance Company. Mr. Shobin has been working in different departments, spending several months at a time in each department, sometimes observing and sometimes actively participating in department activities. Mr. Shobin is participating in the development technique known as **plateauing / job rotation / programmed instruction.**

36. Draw a line from the off-the-job training method listed in the left-hand column to the appropriate objectives described in the right-hand column.

Role playing	This method is used to generate solutions to problems or to gain an understanding of new techniques or information.
Case studies	This method teaches employees to use logical, systematic approaches to resolving problems and it enhances decision-making skills.
Conference method	This method enables employees to try out newly learned interpersonal skills and communication techniques.

37. List four types of off-the-job programs that companies use for employee development.

(1) ______________________________

(2) ______________________________

(3) ______________________________

(4) ______________________________

EVALUATING STAFF PERFORMANCE

38. Circle the word that correctly completes the following sentence:

Documentation is a(n) (increasingly/decreasingly) important aspect of the performance appraisal system.

* * *

39a. Identify one benefit and three drawbacks to using the essay appraisal method of employee evaluation.

Benefit ______________________________

Drawback #1 ______________________________

Drawback #2____

Drawback #3____

39b. ____ True or False? To offset its limitations, the essay appraisal technique is often used with a more structured technique.

* * *

40. The following cases give information about performance appraisals given to four different employees. Based on the information given, determine the method of performance appraisal that is being described and write that method next to the description.

___________ Julia's supervisor keeps a record of Julia's good and bad work behavior and uses these examples to judge Julia's performance at the end of the evaluation period.

___________ Quincy's manager augments the standardized performance appraisal form by writing a report about Quincy's job performance, strengths, weaknesses, and accomplishments.

___________ Adam receives from his manager a form that lists characteristics that relate to job performance and notes that the manager has circled "highly effective" next to "cooperates with fellow workers" and "satisfactory" next to "finds better ways to do work."

___________ Zelda's supervisor lists all five employees in her work group and identifies the employee who best typifies the characteristic "completes work quickly." Then the supervisor identifies the employee who least typifies the same characteristic. She continues this process until all five employees are placed in order from best to worst with respect to the characteristic.

41. Circle the words in parentheses that correctly complete the following sentence:

Behaviorally anchored rating scales are similar to graphic rating scales; however, while BARS have (more/less) detail, the graphic rating scale is (harder/easier) to complete.

SEPARATION OF EMPLOYEES

42. List four ways in which an employee and an organization may separate.

(1)________________ (2)________________

(3)________________ (4)________________

43. Information garnered from exit interviews is often circulated to managers and supervisors throughout an organization. How may this information be useful?

____

____

44. ____ True or False? A company's outplacement counseling to an employee who has been separated from the company indicates that the company is assuming responsibility for finding the person new employment.

45. When certain types of separations occur in unusually large numbers, such activity can indicate specific problems in an organization. State one or more specific problems that may be present as evidenced by a large number of separations of each of the following types.

Resignations________________

Layoffs________________

Discharges________________

ESTABLISHING COMPENSATION SYSTEMS

46. In order to develop an equitable pay scale, a company must complete job evaluations of all jobs in the company by analyzing and rating each job according to a number of factors. Identify four such factors.

(1)________________ (2)________________

(3)________________ (4)________________

* * *

47a. Once an equitable job evaluation system is established, a company can develop wage and salary scales. What factor in a unionized workplace may affect the wages paid for a job?

____

47b. Where can a company find comparative pay information?

____

47c. What two government requirements affect a company's wage and salary policies? Explain.

____

____

* * *

48. Decide whether each of the following statements about pay incentive plans is true or false. Place **"T"** for true or **"F"** for false beside each statement.

____ Some incentive plans reward employees for their individual work with a production bonus that is a percentage of the employee's hourly wage or annual salary.

____ When an employee with a deferred profit-sharing plan retires, he or she is paid the deferred profits, plus the interest or dividends earned on those profits.

____ In companies with an employee stock ownership plan (ESOP), the company sells a certain percentage of its stock each year and makes a contribution to each eligible employee's pension account.

49. Identify four benefits and services commonly provided to a company's employees over and above their normal wages and salaries.

(1) ____________________ (2) ____________________

(3) ____________________ (4) ____________________

To assess your understanding of the material in this chapter, go to the Test Preparation Guide (TPG) for this course and work the sample questions from this chapter. The TPG will explain how to study for and take examinations and will provide you with practice in answering the types of questions that appear on FLMI examinations. Be sure to check your answers to see how well you have mastered the material covered in this chapter. If you have not mastered the material, then reread the chapter in the assigned textbook and rework the corresponding exercises in this student guide. Then return to the TPG and rework the sample questions provided.

Chapter 16

The Information Systems Function

To help you prepare for the FLMI examination for this course, read the entire preface of this student guide. It contains many practical pointers that will help you in studying FLMI educational material. This student guide is designed to help you learn the material covered in the assigned textbook. Working the exercises in this student guide is not a substitute for reading the book. Be sure to read the assigned chapter in the book before completing the exercises in the corresponding chapter of the student guide. Consult the current LOMA Insurance Education Catalog for the correct text assignment for this course.

CHAPTER OVERVIEW

A system that collects, processes, and distributes information is one of an insurance company's most important assets. Chapter 16 described the components of an information system and discussed automated office systems. You read about the organization of the information systems function and its relationships with other departments. You also learned about typical insurance company systems.

After studying this chapter, you should be able to

- Describe the components of an information system and an insurance company's sources of data for such a system
- Explain the data base concept and its importance to insurance company operations
- Discuss some recent developments in office systems technology
- Identify the different responsibilities of people who work in the information systems area
- Describe the purpose of a decision support system
- Describe the operations of typical insurance company information systems, including the information systems used by a company's different functional areas

Outline of Major Topics Covered in this Chapter

I. The Importance of an Effective Information System

II. Information Systems
   A. Input, Processing, Output, and Control
   B. Internal and External Information Needs
III. Data Base and Data Communications
   A. Data Bases
      1. Decision support applications
   B. Data Communications Networks
      1. Data communications applications
IV. Automated Office Systems
   A. Image Processing
   B. Electronic Publishing
V. Organization of the Information Systems Department
   A. The Information Systems Staff
      1. Operations
      2. Systems analysis
      3. Programming
      4. Data administration
VI. Relationships with Other Departments
   A. Training
   B. Technical Assistance
      1. Decision support systems
      2. Expert systems
   C. Assistance in Equipment Purchase Decisions
VII. Typical Insurance Company Systems
   A. Producing Ledger Proposals
   B. Processing Insurance Policy Applications
   C. Daily Cycle System
   D. Other Information Systems
      1. Marketing
      2. Actuarial
      3. Underwriting
      4. Customer service
      5. Claim administration
      6. Investments
      7. Accounting
      8. Legal
      9. Human resources

Review of Key Terms and Concepts

Define the following key terms and concepts:

information system (p. 453)____

____

input (p. 454)____

____

processing (p. 454)____

____

output (p. 454)____

____

control (p. 454)____

____

operational information (p. 454)_________________________________

____

management information (p. 455)__________________________________

____

data base (p. 455)____

____

nonredundant data (p. 456)_______________________________________

____

data communications (p. 457)_____________________________________

____

dumb terminal (p. 458)____

____

intelligent terminal (p. 458)____________________________________

____

automated office systems (p. 458)________________________________

____

image processing (p. 459)____

____

electronic publishing (p. 460)___________________________________

____

end user (p. 461)____

____

systems analyst (p. 462)____

____

programmer (p. 462)____

____

data administration (DA) (p. 463)_______________________________

____

decision support system (DSS) (p. 465)__________________________

____

expert system (p. 465)____

____

ledger proposal (p. 469)____

____

alpha system (p. 469)____

____

daily cycle system (p. 470)_____________________________________

____

marketing information system (p. 471)___________________________

____

WORKING OUTLINE

Information Systems

1. Different insurance company information system functions are described in the left-hand column on the next page. Draw a line from each description in the left-hand column to the name of the function in the right-hand column that the description represents.

The total amount of premiums received for the month is generated	Input
All of the premium payment amounts are totalled	Processing
The amount of each premium payment that was received during the month is entered into the system	Output
The operation is monitored to ensure that all data is processed as specified and made available only to those people with proper access	Control

2. The data an insurance company uses comes from the company's various operating units as well as from sources outside the company. List four of the most common sources of internal data and give an example of each.

   (1) ______________________________

   (2) ______________________________

   (3) ______________________________

   (4) ______________________________

   Give some examples of sources of data outside the company.

   ____

3. From the following list, circle the organizations and individuals that need information from an insurance company:

financial institutions	policyowners	consumer groups
regulatory agencies	stockholders	prospects

Data Base and Data Communications

4. The data that is contained in a data base must be essential to the continuing operation of one or more particular functions of the company. Why should nonessential data not be stored in a data base?

   ____

5. The Tabular Life Insurance Company has developed a data base that includes data from all areas of the company. Formerly, each department processed only the data required for its own files, which were physically and electronically separate from the files

of other departments. State one major benefit to Tabular's staff of the new form of data base.

____

6. ____ True or False? When a data base is established, all data must be combined into one huge file.

7. The Pavilion Life Insurance Company's data base is organized into related files that are connected through a master file. Briefly describe a typical policyowner data base, and identify some files that are typically related or interconnected.

____

____

8. ____ True or False? In a properly constructed data base, files that are used for one department are automatically updated for all departments when any one department changes the data.

9. Lynn Worth is the chief financial officer of the Guidance Life Insurance Company. What information can Mr. Worth obtain through Guidance's data base from each of the following departments to enable him to compare the company's actual and expected cash flows?

marketing________________________________

accounting________________________________

investments________________________________

10. Circle the phrase in parentheses that correctly completes the following passage.

The Global Life Insurance Company needs fast transmission of information from their New York office to their London and Hong Kong offices. Global's ideal system would be linked through (direct electronic links/radio wave transmission).

11. Chuck Wilson, a field office agent for the Attachment Life Insurance Company, can provide much more efficient customer service since Attachment installed its data communications network. Cite two ways that the new network can help Chuck to improve customer service.

(1)____

(2)____

12. Data communications networks link insurers directly to many sources of useful information outside the company. Give five examples of such external information sources that can be accessed electronically.

(1)____

(2)____

(3)____

(4)____

(5)____

Automated Office Systems

13. Circle the specific automation technologies that were introduced into most insurance company offices during the 1970s and 1980s:

word processing   teleconferencing   facsimile (FAX) transmissions

electronic mail   mimeographing and copying paper documents   mainframe computing

Identify two relatively new office systems that are beginning to appear in insurance companies.

(1) ____________________ (2) ____________________

14. Circle the words in parentheses that correctly complete the following sentence:

The (increasing/decreasing) use of image processing technology is (increasing/reducing) the number of paper files that insurance companies maintain.

15. Image processing offers several benefits to insurers over traditional paper files. Discuss each of the following benefits:

immediate retrieval______________________________

____

space saving__________________________________

____

improved security______________________________

____

enhanced information ______________________________

____

16. Insurance companies are increasingly using electronic publishing technology. An electronic publishing system is able to

combine the following inputs ______________________________

process these inputs into ______________________________,

and

output the result onto ______________________________.

17. Write a "C" beside each statement that correctly characterizes the features of electronic publishing.

____ It can produce attractive customized proposals for potential policyowners or group policyholders.

____ It can produce policies electronically in an agent's or broker's office and make any necessary revisions.

____ It can identify prospective policyowners and group policyholders.

____ It can issue checks with a company logo, check serial numbers, and other necessary data.

____ It can create policy forms that can be modified without undue delay.

____ It can determine from a preprinted policy application whether an applicant for life insurance presents excessive mortality risk.

____ It can save storage costs by printing materials only in the quantity needed.

Organization of the Information Systems Department

18. Which of the following functions are the responsibility of the IS staff? Circle as many as apply.

developing computer systems	maintaining computer systems
helping end users	operating computer systems
advising other areas about technology	modifying computer systems

Harriet Springer is a systems analyst in an insurance company's IS area. Ms. Springer's current project involves developing a new accounting system for the accounting department.

19a. ____ True or False? Ms. Springer will work with the accounting staff to become thoroughly familiar with the area's functions.

19b. Once Ms. Springer has designed a computerized system to handle the accounting department's functions, she will communicate her plan to

____a control clerk ____a programmer ____a computer operator

19c. Before making the decision to design the new accounting system in-house, Ms. Springer and the accounting manager looked at commercially available systems and programs from outside vendors. Identify two benefits and one drawback of using systems and programs from outside vendors.

benefit #1____

benefit #2____

drawback____

* * *

For the following three questions, indicate with a **"T"** or an **"F"** whether each statement is true or false.

20. ____ The roles of systems analyst and programmer are becoming less distinct; sometimes the same person, called a programmer/analyst, performs both functions.

21. ____ Programmers write programs in special computer languages because natural languages contain ambiguous words.

22. ____ Most insurance company programmers choose a single computer language and then use only that language.

* * *

23. ____ True or False? Depending on company size, the data administration (DA) function might be performed by a single person or a group of persons.

Relationships with Other Departments

24. Circle the word that correctly completes the following sentence:

There is a trend in recent years for the IS department staff to communicate (more/less) with other departments.

25. Identify two possible arrangements by which computer experts are assigned to help people in other departments to use computer technology.

(1)____

(2)____

26. Briefly describe these three types of training generally offered by an IS department to other company employees.

Formal instruction________________________________

____

Walk-in assistance________________________________

____

"Hot-line" assistance_____________________________

____

27. How do desktop or personal computers (PCs) help people to perform their work more efficiently?

____

____

28. A decision support system (DSS) may provide access to a number of internal and external information sources that can enable a company's executives and managers to make informed decisions. Circle the kinds of information that may be accessed by a DSS:

operations information	personnel information
external data bases	economic reports
stock and bond market reports	news retrieval services

29. ____ True or False? Expert systems make decisions based on their own form of logic, which is significantly different from the logic used by human decision-makers.

30. Circle the word(s) in parentheses that correctly completes the following sentence:

An expert system is particularly well-suited to functions in the insurance industry that (do/do not) require repetitive applications of corporate policies and procedures.

31. Identify four insurance functions for which expert systems are used.

(1)____________________ (2)____________________

(3)____________________ (4)____________________

* * *

32a. The Micropolis Life Insurance Company uses an expert system in its underwriting function. Given the proper input, what underwriting tasks can this expert system be expected to perform?

____

____

____

32b. Place an **"X"** beside the benefits that Micropolis can achieve with its expert underwriting system.

____ The system can perform risk selection many times faster than a human employee.

____ The system can free experienced underwriters to work on complex cases that do not meet the constraints of the system.

____ The system can result in cost savings to Micropolis because of its processing speed.

____ The system's underwriting results are more consistent than they would be if performed by people.

* * *

33. ____ True or False? All company employees are expected to become informed about technological advances that may affect their own functional areas and to approach IS specialists only at the actual time of equipment purchase.

Typical Insurance Company Systems

34. Why can preprinted rate manuals not be used for investment-based products?

____

How do ledger proposal systems overcome the limitations of preprinted rate manuals?

____

35. Place an **"L"** beside each kind of equipment that may be used to produce a ledger proposal.

____ an agent's laptop computer

____ a personal computer in the agent's office

____ the mainframe system in the home office

36. Once an application for insurance is sent to the home office, it is entered into the alpha system. The alpha system will alert the underwriter if the applicant has

(1) ______________________________ or (2) ______________________________

37. Circle the devices used to enter information into the daily cycle system.

optical scanners   terminals   other electronic data entry devices

38. Describe information that the daily cycle system master records contains regarding each policy's

insured ____

actuarial information ____________________________________

____

39. ____ True or False? The most common function performed by the daily cycle system is updating address information.

40. Identify several types of information contained in a marketing information system.

(1) ______________________________ (2) ______________________________

(3) ______________________________ (4) ______________________________

41. Circle the word that correctly completes the following sentence:

The actuarial department is probably the (most/least) calculation-intensive area in an insurance company.

42. Briefly explain why an information system is particularly crucial to an actuarial department.

____

____

43. Circle the word that correctly completes the following sentence:

Because the data base of underwriting impairment information may be (large/small), insurers may merge their data bases with other insurers.

44. An effective customer service information system is designed to

(1) ______________________________

(2) ______________________________

(3) ______________________________

(4) ______________________________

45. Circle the word that correctly completes the following sentence:

The greatest efficiencies in a computerized claim payment system are realized in systems that handle a (large/small) volume of claims.

46. ____ True or False? Information access to the Medical Information Bureau (MIB) is especially useful to claim personnel in detecting fraud and overinsurance.

47. ____ True or False? Computers allow investment specialists to determine the worth of the company's investments based on a number of scenarios.

48. Information system capabilities enable accountants to code accounts so that they are tied directly to regulatory authorities' reporting requirements. How else may this same information be used?

____

49. Identify two commercially available electronic data bases containing legal information.

(1) ______________ (2) ______________

What kinds of information can a legal staff member obtain from these data bases?

____

To assess your understanding of the material in this chapter, go to the Test Preparation Guide (TPG) for this course and work the sample questions from this chapter. The TPG will explain how to study for and take examinations and will provide you with practice in answering the types of questions that appear on FLMI examinations. Be sure to check your answers to see how well you have mastered the material covered in this chapter. If you have not mastered the material, then reread the chapter in the assigned textbook and rework the corresponding exercises in this student guide. Then return to the TPG and rework the sample questions provided.

Chapter 17

International Operations of Life and Health Insurers

To help you prepare for the FLMI examination for this course, read the entire preface of this student guide. It contains many practical pointers that will help you in studying FLMI educational material. This student guide is designed to help you learn the material covered in the assigned textbook. Working the exercises in this student guide is not a substitute for reading the book. Be sure to read the assigned chapter in the book before completing the exercises in the corresponding chapter of the student guide. Consult the current LOMA Insurance Education Catalog for the correct text assignment for this course.

CHAPTER OVERVIEW

North American life and health insurers are increasingly expanding their operations to foreign countries. Insurers from Asia and Europe are also finding opportunities to enter other marketplaces. Chapter 17 examined the motivations for such expansion and the factors an insurer considers when starting international operations. You learned about organization structures used in international operations and the marketing and staffing considerations of such operations. You also read about the effects of international operations on both the host country and the insurer's home country.

After studying this chapter, you should be able to

- Describe different approaches to international insurance operations
- Discuss motivations that an insurer would have to market its products internationally
- Describe staffing, marketing, and organizational issues that an insurer has to face when beginning to operate internationally
- List and explain some potential benefits and drawbacks of international insurance operations

Outline of Major Topics Covered in this Chapter

I. Parties Involved in International Business
   A. Attitudes of Multinational Corporations

II. Motivations to Operate Internationally
  A. Marketing Opportunities
    1. New markets
    2. Gaining a competitive edge
  B. Financial Opportunities
    1. Types of business risk
  C. Other Incentives to Operate Internationally
III. Factors to Consider in Starting International Operations
  A. Methods of Undertaking Foreign Operations
    1. Branch offices and subsidiaries
    2. Joint ventures
    3. Acquisitions
  B. Organizational Structures
  C. Staffing Considerations
    1. Host country staffing
    2. Home country staffing
    3. Other methods of staffing international operations
  D. Marketing Considerations
IV. Effects of International Insurance Operations
  A. Effects on the Host Country
  B. Effects on the Home Country

Review of Key Terms and Concepts

Define the following key terms and concepts:

multinational corporation (MNC) (p. 478)______________________________

____

host country (p. 478)____

____

home country (p. 478)____

____

ethnocentric attitude (p. 478)____

____

polycentric attitude (p. 478)____

____

geocentric attitude (p. 478)____

____

political risk (p. 485)____

____

joint venture (p. 490)____

____

economies of scale (p. 490)____

____

host country staffing (p. 494)____

____

home country staffing (p. 495)____

____

third-country national (p. 496)____

____

polycentric staffing (p. 496)____

____

WORKING OUTLINE

1. Cite one benefit and one drawback of an ethnocentric attitude among managers of a company with international operations.

   benefit____

   drawback____

2. Circle the words that correctly complete the following passage:

   A company whose management has a polycentric attitude toward its international business will use host country employees (extensively/minimally). A polycentric approach may help an insurer's products and operations fit local conditions (more/less) closely than would an ethnocentric approach. Control of international operations is (easier/harder) with the polycentric approach than with other approaches.

3. ____ True or False? Managers with a geocentric attitude focus their efforts on using the most effective techniques and practices, regardless of whether they are based on home country ideas or host country ideas.

Motivations to Operate Internationally

For insurance, as for any business, the basic motivation for operating is to earn an acceptable return on money invested by its owners or stockholders.

4. Circle the word that correctly completes the following sentence:

   When insurance has been marketed for a long time in a particular country or region, the market for insurance there is said to be

   immature   emerging   mature

5. From time to time, local economic or political changes occur in an area that make the area a good new market for a foreign insurer's products and services. Give an example of a country or region that, in your opinion, currently presents promising marketing opportunities for life and health insurers. Explain your answer.

   ____

   ____

   ____

   ____

6. Circle the words that correctly complete the following sentence:

   Throughout the world, people are becoming (more/less) sophisticated about financial products, thus creating a (more/less) positive outlook for the globalization of the insurance business.

==

NOTE TO STUDENTS: THE NEXT FEW SECTIONS OF THIS CHAPTER REFER TO A FICTIONAL COMPANY, THE WIDEWORLD INSURANCE COMPANY.

*   *   *

7a. The Wideworld Insurance Company, whose home country is the United States, plans to introduce its products and services into a number of foreign countries. Place an "X" beside each benefit that Wideworld may gain from entering foreign markets.

   ____ A market for products that cannot be sold in the United States because of legal constraints

   ____ A chance to gauge the market potential for new products

   ____ An opportunity to learn more about other insurers that are Wideworld's competitors now or that may become its competitors in the future

____ A chance to test marketing techniques on a smaller scale before using them in the United States

____ A chance to experiment with alternative distribution methods

____ The ability to keep up with competition that has already opened up in these host countries

7b. When Wideworld begins operating overseas, what factors could favorably affect its overall financial performance?

____

____

____

7c. Briefly explain how moving into several different countries can help Wideworld to diversify the following types of risk:

underwriting risk____

____

economic risk____

____

political risk____

____

* * *

8. ____ True or False? International operations can offer testing grounds for ambitious employees at every level and can offer challenge to managers and executives.

Factors to Consider in Starting International Operations

9. In order to prepare for international operations, Wideworld needs to do research in a wide variety of areas. For each of the following topics, give two questions that Wideworld's planners should have answered before the company begins to sell insurance policies internationally.

market potential____

____

regulatory climate____

____

taxes____

____

investments____

____

10. Identify several other factors that Wideworld would consider when planning to enter foreign markets.

__________________________ __________________________

__________________________ __________________________

__________________________ __________________________

11. ____ True or False? Establishing branch offices overseas would give Wideworld less control over its international activities than any other organizational method of entering foreign markets.

12. ____ True or False? If Wideworld should choose to establish subsidiary companies overseas, it could oversee the operations directly.

13. Two considerations that might lead Wideworld to choose a joint venture with a company already operating in a foreign market rather than setting up a branch office or a subsidiary are

(1) _______________________ (2)___________________________

14. What would motivate a company already operating in a host country to help Wideworld gain entry into the host's market through a joint venture? State three possible motivations.

(1) ____

(2) ____

(3) ____

15. Each statement below refers to a potential joint venture between Wideworld and a host country partner. Beside each statement, indicate whether the statement is true or false by writing a **"T"** for true or an **"F"** for false in the space provided.

____ Both companies could benefit from economies of scale.

____ The two companies would share the risk involved in such an alliance.

____ In a joint venture, Wideworld would probably face more stringent regulation from local authorities than if it entered the market on its own.

____ Wideworld increases its chances of making social or linguistic mistakes by working so closely with a host company partner.

____ Both companies would benefit from having a single source of management control.

16. In researching other ways to enter a foreign market, Wideworld is also considering the acquisition of a company already based in the host country. Identify two benefits to Wideworld of such an acquisition.

    (1) ____

    (2) ____

    What two possible situations in the host country might prevent Wideworld's acquisition of a company already based there?

    (1) ____

    (2) ____

17. Identify the international organizational structure represented in each of the following situations by writing **"G"** for geographical, **"F"** for functional, **"P"** for product-based, or **"M"** for matrix beside each statement.

____ Joseph Warren is Vice President, Marketing, and Marty Barranco is Vice President, South American Operations, for Cosmos Life Insurance Co. As such, the two Vice Presidents share some responsibilities for Cosmos Life's marketing in South America.

____ Friedrich Heinz is the vice president over whole life products for all of Megalife's European operations. Reporting to him are managers of whole life products in each of the five European countries in which Megalife operates.

____ Marcia Hernandez is senior vice president in charge of Wideworld's entire operation in Spain.

____ Ed Jahreis heads GlobalView's claims activities throughout its Italian operations.

==

18. ____ True or False? How an insurer staffs its international operations depends upon whether the insurer follows an ethnocentric, geocentric, or polycentric approach to business.

19. Decide whether each of the following statements best describes home country staffing or host country staffing by placing an "X" in the appropriate column beside each statement.

	Home Country Staffing	**Host Country Staffing**
The insurer becomes acclimated to local manners and ways of doing business more quickly.		
The work force is less expensive to hire and maintain.		
The home office has greater control over the operations.		
Language barriers exist within the organization.		
Communications between the home office and the foreign operation are better.		
The company risks losing employees who do not adapt well to the host country.		

20. Briefly discuss the benefits and drawbacks involved when a company entering foreign markets relies solely on third-country nationals to staff its office.

____

____

____

21. ____ True or False? Probably the most sensible approach to staffing an international operation that is projected to be a long-term venture is ethnocentric staffing.

22. What questions should an insurer ask with regard to marketing considerations when entering a foreign market? Cite at least two questions for each of the four "Ps."

product____

____

promotion______________________________________

____

pricing____

____

place (physical distribution)__________________________

____

Effects of International Insurance Operations

23. Discuss benefits that can accrue to the host country from international operations within its borders, with regard to

capital inflow___________________________________

career opportunities______________________________

What problems might international operations bring into a host country?

(1) ____

(2) ____

24. Identify a benefit and a drawback of international operations to the home country.

benefit____

drawback_______________________________________

To assess your understanding of the material in this chapter, go to the <u>Test Preparation Guide</u> (TPG) for this course and work the sample questions from this chapter. The TPG will explain how to study for and take examinations and will provide you with practice in answering the types of questions that appear on FLMI examinations. Be sure to check your answers to see how well you have mastered the material covered in this chapter. If you have not mastered the material, then reread the chapter in the assigned textbook and rework the corresponding exercises in this student guide. Then return to the TPG and rework the sample questions provided.

Chapter 18

Professionalism in the Insurance Industry

To help you prepare for the FLMI examination for this course, read the entire preface of this student guide. It contains many practical pointers that will help you in studying FLMI educational material. This student guide is designed to help you learn the material covered in the assigned textbook. Working the exercises in this student guide is not a substitute for reading the book. Be sure to read the assigned chapter in the book before completing the exercises in the corresponding chapter of the student guide. Consult the current LOMA Insurance Education Catalog for the correct text assignment for this course.

CHAPTER OVERVIEW

Professionalism in its employees is very important to the quality of products and services that a life and health insurance company offers. Chapter 18 discussed the ethical behavior upon which professionalism is based. You learned about the importance of corporate ethics and the establishment of ethical codes. You read about professional education programs that are available to life and health insurance employees, and you were introduced to company and professional associations. The chapter concluded with a brief discussion of the importance of professionalism.

After studying this chapter, you should be able to

- Describe the difficulties inherent in defining ethical behavior
- Discuss the importance of corporate ethics and the establishment of ethical codes
- Describe types of professional education and training available to employees in the life and health insurance industry
- Identify associations that serve the life and health insurance industry

Outline of Major Topics Covered in this Chapter

I. Characteristics of Professionalism
II. Ethical Behavior
    A. Importance of Corporate Ethics
    B. Ethical Codes

III. Education and Training
    A. Insurance Education Programs
        1. The FLMI Insurance Education Program
        2. CLU and ChFC professional education programs
        3. ASA and FSA professional education programs
        4. The HIAA Education Program
        5. The ICA Claims Education Program
        6. The AALU/FALU education program
    B. Career Counseling
IV. Company Associations and Professional Associations
    A. Company Associations
        1. American Council of Life Insurance (ACLI)
        2. Canadian Life and Health Insurance Association (CLHIA)
        3. LOMA (Life Office Management Association)
        4. LIMRA (Life Insurance Marketing and Research Association)
        5. Health Insurance Association of America (HIAA)
        6. National Association of Life Companies (NALC)
    B. Professional Associations
V. The Importance of Professionalism

Review of Key Term

Define the following key term:

ethical behavior (p. 501)____

____

WORKING OUTLINE

Ethical Behavior

1. ____ True or False? Truly ethical behavior requires not only an adherence to ethical standards, but also an adherence to the spirit of ethical behavior in questionable or borderline situations.

2. Circle the word that correctly completes the following sentence:

   Insurance sales agents who engage in the practice of churning are engaging in (ethical/unethical) behavior.

3. Briefly discuss the importance of ethical behavior among

   a corporation and its customers______________________________

   ____

   a corporation and its employees______________________________

   ____

4. Does your company have a written policy on business ethics and conduct? Does your company have an unwritten ethics policy? Describe the policy (or these policies) in general.

____

____

____

5. Describe a corporation's typical ethical codes. How can these codes help employees to resolve ethical dilemmas?

____

____

Education and Training

6. How does employees' participation in education and training throughout their careers benefit

the employees themselves?______________________________

the employer?______________________________________

7. Match the professional designation on the left with the most appropriate description of its general course content on the right. Write the number of the appropriate description in the space provided in the left-hand column.

	Designation		Description
____	FLMI	(1)	claim administration as well as a general introduction to life and health insurance
____	ALHC	(2)	financial planning and life insurance sales
____	ASA, FSA	(3)	home office underwriting as well as general insurance and business topics
____	HIA	(4)	insurance and functional operations of insurance companies as well as areas of general business interest
____	AALU, FALU	(5)	actuarial study as well as general mathematics, probability and statistics, life contingencies, valuation of assets, and other subjects
____	CLU, ChFC	(6)	individual health insurance and group life and health insurance

8. ____ True or False? Insurance education opportunities that are available to insurance company employees are most useful when pursued as part of an overall career plan.

9. Circle the phrase that correctly completes the following sentence:

A career plan that is developed together by an individual employee and a designated human resources specialist or the employee's manager is usually intended to foresee the roles that the employee may play in the company over a period of the next

six months **year to eighteen months** **ten to fifteen years**

10. How does a company utilize a skills inventory in conjunction with career counseling?

____

Company Associations and Professional Associations

11. Differentiate briefly between a company association and a professional association.

____

____

12. Match the company association on the left with the most appropriate description of that association on the right. Write the number of the appropriate description in the space provided in the left-hand column.

____ CLHIA	(1)	represents the life insurance business in legislative and regulatory areas at all areas of U.S. government
____ NALC	(2)	provides life and health insurance information as the primary source of such information in Canada
____ LIMRA	(3)	promotes management excellence in life and health insurance companies and other financial institutions through seminars, workshops, and insurance education programs
____ LOMA	(4)	works to improve life insurance distribution efficiency, conducts research, offers consulting services, and provides marketing management educational services
____ HIAA	(5)	helps its 300-plus member companies in the United States and Canada promote and develop voluntary health insurance
____ ACLI		

13. In what ways can employee membership in professional associations benefit both the employee and his or her employer?

(1) ______________________________

(2) ______________________________

(3) ______________________________

(4) ______________________________

(5) ______________________________

14. Identify and briefly describe one or more professional associations specific to insurance company

actuaries ______________________________

____

underwriters ______________________________

____

attorneys ______________________________

____

financial planners and insurance sales professionals ______________________________

____

15. Briefly describe the mission of FLMI Societies.

____

____

To assess your understanding of the material in this chapter, go to the Test Preparation Guide (TPG) for this course and work the sample questions from this chapter. The TPG will explain how to study for and take examinations and will provide you with practice in answering the types of questions that appear on FLMI examinations. Be sure to check your answers to see how well you have mastered the material covered in this chapter. If you have not mastered the material, then reread the chapter in the assigned textbook and rework the corresponding exercises in this student guide. Then return to the TPG and rework the sample questions provided.

Student Survey

on

FLMI Course 2

Life and Health Insurance Company Operations

We want to make this course and its study materials better. In fact, we want to make them the best course and study materials available for insurance industry personnel on the subject of Life and Health Insurance Company Operations. But we need you to make them the best. Please help us by completing the following survey and returning it to LOMA, Education Division, 5770 Powers Ferry Road, Atlanta, GA 30327, Attention: FLMI Course 2 Survey. Fill in the blanks and circle the answers that best reflect your opinion.

Questions 1-5 refer to the Student Guide for this course.

1. In preparing for the FLMI Course 2 examination, what percentage of the Student Guide did you complete? (Circle the approximate answer.)

   100% ------- 75% ------- 50% ------- 25% ------- 0%

2. How did you use the Student Guide? (Check all answers that apply.)

   ___ Read the Chapter Overview in the Student Guide

   ___ Reviewed the Learning Objectives in the Student Guide

   ___ Familiarized myself with the Chapter Outline

   ___ Defined the Key Terms and Concepts

   ___ Completed the exercises in the Working Outline

   ___ Other (please describe) ____

   ____

3. How helpful was the Student Guide to your learning of the material?

1 -------------------	2 -----------------	3
Very Helpful	Somewhat Helpful	Not at all Helpful

4. How could the student guide have been more helpful? ______________________

____

5. Overall, the Student Guide's thoroughness in covering the material in the text *Operations of Life and Health Insurance Companies* was (circle your answer):

1	2	3
Too Thorough	About Right	Not Thorough Enough

Questions 6-8 refer to the textbook for this course.

6. The writing style in the text *Operations of Life and Health Insurance Companies* was

1	2	3	4	5
Very easy to understand	Somewhat easy to understand	About average	Somewhat difficult to understand	Very difficult to understand

7. What additional topics should be covered in future editions of the book?

____

____

____

8. What other comments do you have about the book's content, design, or educational value?

____

____

____

Questions 9-13 refer to your preparation for this course's examination.

9. How did you prepare for the FLMI Course 2 examination? (Check all that apply.)

( ) Self-study
( ) Attended formal classes
( ) Used Test Preparation Guide
( ) Reviewed Student Guide prior to examination
( ) Studied with others
( ) Reviewed text prior to examination
( ) Studied from old examination

10. Approximately what percentage of the textbook's assigned chapters did you read?

100% -------- 75% --------- 50% ---------- 25% ---------- 0%

11. Did you sit for the Course 2 exam before completing this survey?

( ) Yes ( ) No

12. If you did sit for the exam, how do you think you did on the exam?

1	2	3
Fairly sure I passed	Maybe I passed/ Maybe I didn't	Fairly sure I did not pass

13. Which FLMI courses had you passed when you enrolled for Course 2?

____ Principles ____ Management ____ Econ./Invest.

____ Law ____ Info. Mgt. ____ Mathematics

____ Marketing ____ Accounting ____ Elective

Questions 14-18 are demographic questions.

14. In what part of your company do you work?

___ home office ___ regional office ___ agency/branch office

15. What is your job level?

____ Administrative/Clerical ____ Supervisor/Manager

____ Technical/Professional ____ Officer/Executive

16. In what functional area of your company do you work?

___ accounting/auditing
___ actuarial
___ administrative services
___ claim administration
___ customer service/policyowner service
___ human resources/personnel/training
___ legal
___ marketing
___ policy issue
___ systems/information resources
___ underwriting
___ investments

___ other ______________________

17. With what type of financial services product(s) do you primarily work? (Check all that apply.)

___ Individual (Ordinary) Life insurance
___ Individual Health - Medical Expense insurance
___ Individual Health - Disability Income insurance
___ Credit Life or Health insurance
___ Group Life insurance
___ Group Health - Medical Expense insurance
___ Group Health - Disability Income insurance
___ Individual Annuities/Individual Retirement Plans
___ Mutual Funds, Limited Partnerships, Real Estate
___ Pension Plans
___ Other (Please list) ______________________________________

18. How would you classify the type of company you work for? (Select one.)

___ Life/Health Insurance Company (Ordinary/Group Lines)
___ Property/Casualty Insurance Company
___ Multi-Line Insurance Company (Life/Health/Property/Casualty)
___ Home Service Insurance Company
___ Combination Insurance Company
___ Fraternal Organization

___ Blue Cross/Blue Shield Company
___ Third Party Administrator/ Administrative Services Organization
___ Health Maintenance Organization
___ Preferred Provider Organization

___ Independent Life/Health Agency or Brokerage Firm
___ Independent Property/Casualty Agency or Brokerage Firm
___ National Brokerage House
___ Independent Marketing Organization

___ Non-Insurance Producer Firm (Bank, Stockbrokerage House, Auto Dealer, Real Estate Agency, Other Financial Institution)
___ Accounting Firm
___ Computer Hardware/Software Company
___ Communications Firm

___ Other (Please indicate) ____

Please complete the following if we may contact you for further information:

Name: ____

Title: ____

Department: ____

Company: ____

Address: ____

____

Telephone: (____) ________________________________

Thank you for completing this survey. Please cut these pages out of the Student Guide and mail them to LOMA, Education Division, 5770 Powers Ferry Road, Atlanta, GA 30327, Attention: Course 2 Survey.